Can God be Trusted?

Can God be Trusted?

GRAHAM MAXWELL

Pineknoll
Publications
REDLANDS, CALIFORNIA

Published by Pine Knoll Publications • 1345 Pine Knoll, Redlands, California 92373 USA

Design & Typography: Linda Wheeler, Win Graphics Prepress

Cover Photograph: Shannon Kirk

Library of Congress Cataloging-in-Publication Data

Maxwell, A. Graham (Arthur Graham), 1921-
  Can God be trusted? / Graham Maxwell.
   p. cm.
  Originally published: Nashville : Southern Pub. Association, 1977.
  ISBN 1-56652-007-X (alk. paper)
  1. God. 2. Apologetics. I. Title.

BT103.M29 2002
239—dc21

              2002035525

CONTENTS

CHAPTER 1
A CRISIS OF TRUST   9

CHAPTER 2
CAN GOD BE TRUSTED?   13

CHAPTER 3
ANGELS WITH GOOD NEWS   21

CHAPTER 4
WHAT IS THE GOOD NEWS?   27

CHAPTER 5
FAITH IN GOD IS NO LEAP IN THE DARK   37

CHAPTER 6
CAN THE BIBLE BE TRUSTED?   47

CHAPTER 7
THE TRUTH ABOUT GOD IN ALL SIXTY-SIX BOOKS   59

CHAPTER 8
WHY DID JESUS HAVE TO DIE?   71

CHAPTER 9
GOD'S RESPECT FOR US SINNERS   85

CHAPTER 10
WORSHIPING GOD WITHOUT FEAR   99

Chapter 11
GOOD NEWS ABOUT THE JUDGMENT   113

CHAPTER 12
A REMINDER OF THE EVIDENCE   127

CHAPTER 13
GOD WAITS FOR US TO TRUST HIM   137

ABOUT THE AUTHOR   147

1   A CRISIS OF TRUST

Behold how good
and pleasant it is when brothers dwell in unity!
—Revised Standard Version

How wonderful it is, how pleasant,
for God's people to live together in harmony!
—Good News Translation

How good, how delightful it is
for all to live together like brothers.
—The Jerusalem Bible

Is there anything more desirable than for people to live together as described in Psalm 133:1? I know of no greater happiness than to be in the company of trusted and trusting friends—all working for the best good of everyone else, no jealousy or suspicion, everyone placing the kindest possible interpretation upon one another's actions and words.

Such unity and goodwill can exist only where there is

complete trust and trustworthiness, mutual love and respect. But the Bible pictures the whole human race as caught up in a great web of distrust. It is all part of the universe-wide crisis of trust that centers around the questioning of the trustworthiness of God himself.

Our infinite God has been accused of untrustworthiness. But God has answered this accusation. And the way he has met the charge is the most convincing evidence of his utter worthiness of our faith.

The Bible is a record of the long and costly demonstration of the trustworthiness of God. If trust could be produced by claims or exhortation, the Bible would be a very different book. But claims of trustworthiness are worth no more than the trustworthiness of the one making them. Thus even when a person has been falsely accused, mere claims or denials prove nothing. Only by the demonstration of trustworthiness over a long period of time and under a variety of circumstances can trustworthiness be convincingly established.

The Bible is generally understood as dealing primarily with God's plan to save sinners. This is certainly included. But a far larger issue is dealt with on the pages of Scripture—the truthfulness and trustworthiness of the Creator himself. The question, Can God be trusted? has been raised in the hearing of the whole onlooking universe. God's answer is as much for them as for us.

This book briefly considers the issues and answers in the great controversy over the character of God. Gracious and convincing teacher that he is, God invites us openly to examine the evidence, to study the entire record—all sixty-six books of the

Bible—and judge for ourselves if the truth is on his side and if we find him worthy of our trust.

The Bible speaks of a special unity that exists among those who have been won back to faith in God. Trusting and admiring the same God, they find that they are able to trust and respect each other. And thus they begin to experience "how wonderful it is, how pleasant, for God's people to live together in harmony!"

CAN GOD BE TRUSTED?

Who would dare to question the integrity of God? Who would dare suggest that God cannot be trusted? Yet with this incredible accusation, the Biblical account of human history begins.

The one who raised this charge had not always been God's enemy. He is pictured first as highly honored, standing in the very presence of our heavenly Father. As God's trusted spokesman he went out among his fellow angels bearing light and truth. He was called "the Light Bearer"—sometimes translated "Lucifer" or "Morning Star"—a name belonging also to the Son of God himself (see Ezekiel 28:14; Isaiah 14:12; 2 Peter 1:19; Revelation 22:16).

But Jesus later called him "a liar and the father of lies" (John 8:44). The last book in the Bible describes him as "that ancient serpent, who is called the Devil and Satan, the deceiver of the whole world" (Revelation 12:9).

"Of course you will not die," the serpent said to Eve. "God knows that as soon as you eat it, your eyes will be opened and you will be like God knowing both good and evil" (Genesis 3:4, 5, NEB, margin). "God has no respect for your freedom and dignity as intelligent individuals," Satan argued. "In selfish tyranny he is depriving you of knowledge and experience that are rightfully yours. He has lied and is not worthy of your trust."

With such falsehoods Satan had already led one third of the angels to side with him against God. Though he is a created being, he had come to think of himself as divine. "'I will ascend to heaven; above the stars of God I will set my throne on high;... I will ascend above the heights of the clouds, I will make myself like the Most High'" (Isaiah 14:13, 14). Insane pride led him later even to ask Jesus, his Creator, to bow down and worship him (Matthew 4:8–10).

To set himself up as God he first must undermine confidence in the One he wished to supplant, and he sought to do this by destroying God's reputation. Since he could find no fault in God, he must resort to deceit.

So began that long struggle for the loyalty of God's free, intelligent creatures. Who was right—God or the brilliant Light Bearer? Could it be true that God was arbitrary and severe, unworthy of the love and trust of the beings he had made? What kind of god would allow his character to be so challenged? Was it strength or weakness that led him to permit such long debate, to allow this controversy to spread throughout his universe?

Finally Satan and his followers even ventured into open revolt. Then God, in his farsighted plan for the best good of all concerned, expelled the rebels from his presence, and the great controversy was extended to the planet on which we live.

As described in the frequently symbolic language of the Book of Revelation, "Then war broke out in heaven. Michael and his angels waged war upon the dragon. The dragon and his angels fought, but they had not the strength to win, and no foothold was left them in heaven. So the great dragon was thrown down, that serpent of old that led the whole world astray, whose name is Satan, or the Devil—thrown down to the earth, and his angels with him.... But woe to you, earth and sea, for the Devil has come down to you in great fury, knowing that his time is short!" (Revelation 12:7–9, 12, NEB).

Some day soon, before Christ returns, Satan will make a last, desperate attempt to win us all to his side. He will appear as an angel of light—the Light Bearer again; Lucifer, the Morning Star (see 2 Corinthians 11:14). He will even proclaim himself to be God. Just as he tried to persuade Christ to worship him in the wilderness of temptation, so he will seek to win our worship now.

The Bible predicts that his efforts will seem to be completely successful. The whole world will worship him—except for a few, "the remnant" (KJV), who will not be deceived. On the contrary, they will take their stand with the loyal angels and maintain their trust in God (see Revelation 12:17; 13:1–8; 14:12).

All of us are unavoidably caught up in this struggle and its results. Throughout history Satan has had vast success in corrupting man's ideas of God. Millions have worshiped deities who use fear and force to have their way. Even among those who call themselves the followers of Christ, the cruelest of persecutions have been conducted in God's name—men and women tortured at the stake to force acceptance of perverted Christian faith.

How often religion has sought to crush man's freedom and deny his sacred right of individuality! How often religion has insulted human dignity, demanding blind submission and belief!

All this bespeaks an arrogant and arbitrary God. Is this the truth that Jesus said would set men free? Or are these Satan's lies about our gracious God? Does God desire the obedience of fear or the obedience that springs from trust and admiration for the rightness of his ways?

No wonder that, for many, God is dead. The deity some have worshiped is perhaps far better dead. But in the vacuum that follows, will worse caricatures of God crowd in to take his place? Man was not designed to live alone, without friends and without God.

What picture do you have of God? Is it the truth? Has it set you free? Do you have friends who rejoice in this same truth, and has it made them people you can trust?

The Bible describes a special unity that exists among those who know and worship God—that is, among those who trust and admire him as he really is. What security, happiness, and peace are to be found in the company of trusted and trusting friends!

I shall never forget the doctors and their team who worked so hard to bring our oldest daughter through a frequently fatal disease. For two months they could offer only guarded hope. But they never had to add that they were doing all they could. Of course they were, and we were glad they knew we knew it.

For years we had known them as the finest experts in their fields and as trusted friends. They all believed in God and spoke freely of their faith. Often we had met for conversation about God, and our shared confidence in him brought great assurance in a time of stress. If our daughter had not been healed, we still would have known that our friends had done everything they could.

I often think of my father and how he would come to the rescue when one of us needed help. I knew I could trust him with my reputation and my life, and both would be as safe in his hands as he could keep them. Even after we had grown up and gone our separate ways, he was ready to go halfway round the world to help in any emergency. And Mother cared just as much. Trustworthy parents make it easier for children to learn to trust in God.

Besides, my father had written more than a hundred books especially to help children, as well as adults, to see how worthy God is of our trust, and we had all grown up with these books. Now we read them to our own children and grandchildren and hope they too will choose to trust. For we must also give them their freedom, if we tell them the truth about God. But though the trust God desires must be individually confirmed as our own, I gratefully realize how much we were helped by our trustworthy parents.

But what of the person for whom the word *father* is anything but a symbol of trustworthiness? In his extraordinary paraphrase of Bible stories entitled *God Is for Real, Man,* Carl Burke, then chaplain of Erie County Jail, New York, tells of trying to assure a boy of God's love by saying, "God is like a father."

"If he's like my father," the boy replied, "I sure would hate him."

Then there was the little girl, abandoned at eight years old on the streets of a large city. She asked him, "If God loves me like you say he does, why did he let Mommy and Daddy go away on me?"

Burke struggled to find something in the lives of these

inner-city children that could symbolize what he wanted to tell them about God. He asked some of them to help him translate parts of the Bible into terms they could understand.

One small boy, who felt that no one in the world had any interest in him at all but who seemed to be longing for someone he could trust, helped paraphrase the twenty-third Psalm. There was only one person who seemed to care, and the boy had come to admire him very much—his probation officer. And so "The Lord is my shepherd" became "The Lord is like my probation officer."

God is the Father of us all, and in his sight we are equally members of his one huge family. But how can he speak to his children, how persuade them to trust, when they think of Father as an aimless drunk and Mother as one who runs around with other men?

How can he hold the trust of his Jewish children who were taught to believe they had no need to fear, for God was with them? They memorized such promises as "I, the Lord your God, hold your right hand; it is I who say to you, 'Fear not, I will help you'" (Isaiah 41:13). Then, in the land where Luther had preached, they watched millions of their people die and heard their neighbors betray them to their enemies.

How can God hold the trust of the gentle people of Cambodia who ran into the streets to welcome their Communist saviors, only to be beaten, shot, and driven by the millions from their homes? In less than two years, between one and two million of Cambodia's seven million people may have died. "There is no love anywhere," one young refugee is reported to have said (see *Murder of a Gentle Land*, condensed in the *Reader's Digest*, 1977). And the men behind the guns made no secret of their scorn for faith in

God. How can the people of that ravished land ever be able to trust God and their fellowmen again?

As the Bible describes our beginning, this world was to be a place of perfect freedom and security. Trusting each other and trusting God, what would there be to fear? But the enemy of God is our enemy too. The one who would deceive us into distrusting God works also to destroy our trust in each other and our own trustworthiness. And where there is no mutual trust and love, there is no real freedom, no real security.

Yet these are the things in life we all desire the most. How good we feel when in times of emergency we show what friends we could always be! How pleased we are when countries work together to rush medicine and food to a neighbor struck by some natural disaster! The whole world applauds when the ship of one nation steams to the rescue of another—especially when it flies the flag of an old enemy. How the world was moved to watch that rare moment of unity in respect and grief when the leaders of the nations stood together at the grave of John F. Kennedy!

If only universal trust could somehow be restored, then we could enjoy again that peaceful assurance that comes with faith in God and confidence in each other. Then we could feel once more that vital sense of dignity and self-respect that come with knowing that God and our friends can safely place their confidence in us.

But we have lost so much of our ability and willingness to trust. Besides, the risk of trusting sometimes seems too great. So often we have let each other down. And with loss of trust in each other, we may begin to wonder if it is even safe to trust in God.

Can God really be trusted? No mere claim can settle this

question. The devil has made many claims, and with impressive authority and power. What is required is the truth, the truth about God. We can not, dare not, trust someone we do not know.

But can God be known that well? As the Infinite One, has he revealed himself in such a way that we may understand and be confident that this is the truth? Does what we see and hear about him add up to such weight of evidence that we can say, "Indeed you can trust God"?

The Bible points forward to a time of worldwide peace, a day when love and trust will fill God's whole universe. Then " 'no longer shall each man teach his neighbor and each his brother, saying, "Know the Lord," for they shall all know me, from the least of them to the greatest, says the Lord' " (Jeremiah 31:34).

This time has not yet come. There are still many neighbors and brothers who do not know God as he is. In ignorance, or blinded by Satan's lies, how can they decide about God? And how can they meet the last worldwide effort to deceive?

It should be no surprise to hear our Lord explain that the gospel must go to all the world before the end can come (Matthew 24:14). God would not ask anyone to face the final, indescribable time of distress without a chance to prepare (see Daniel 12:1–3).

As a schoolboy I always considered it an honor when my teacher would ask me to deliver an important item of news. The more important the news, the greater the privilege of telling. It is the inestimable privilege of those who have already made up their minds to trust God, now to spread the Good News, the everlasting truth about our gracious and trustworthy God.

3   ANGELS WITH GOOD NEWS

More than nineteen hundred years have passed since Jesus asked his followers to take the gospel to all the world. When that is done, he said, then the end will come (Matthew 24:14).

The truth that the Son of God had come to reveal was not to be guarded as a secret known only by a privileged few. Some of the most popular religions in Jesus' day, known as the Mysteries, were built around sacred information disclosed only to those who had passed through special rites of initiation.

But *gospel* means "good news," and as such it was to be publicly made known. Jesus directed that it be given the widest possible circulation, even as far as "the end of the earth" (Acts 1:8), to "all nations" (Matthew 28:19), "to the whole creation" (Mark 16:15). As far as Satan's lies had gone, so should go the truth.

The small band of Christian believers set out confidently to fulfill this immense assignment. They even expected to complete it in a very short time. Had not Jesus indicated that he would be coming back soon? Had he not warned them to be constantly on the watch lest they be unprepared for his return and he catch them by surprise? Some believers in Thessalonica even stopped working, in the mistaken belief that the end had already come. Paul had to inform them that there were still some important events yet to take place before Christ would return (2 Thessalonians 2:1–12; 3:6–13).

But a whole generation passed, and still the Lord had not come. Now only John was left of the original twelve apostles, and he was imprisoned on the lonely Isle of Patmos. Had something gone wrong? The Good News had been well received by many. But it had also provoked serious and sometimes violent opposition. Many Christians had even been killed by the very people they were trying to help.

But, much more seriously, some believers were beginning to doubt the truthfulness of the Good News they had been trying to spread. Some were now even denying that the Son of God had really come in human form to bring the truth about his Father (2 John 7).

At this critical moment God sent another message of encouragement and explanation. To the elderly prisoner on the Isle of Patmos he sent the information recorded in the last book of the New Testament. John described it as "the revelation of Jesus Christ, which God gave him to show to his servants what must soon take place" (Revelation 1:1).

This message advised Christians to take a larger view of life than just the difficulties of the moment. The individual believer must understand that he has become actively involved in the great controversy between Christ and Satan, a conflict that involves the whole universe.

For the first time in the Bible mention is made of the war long ago up in heaven and the extent of Satan's influence among the angels (see Revelation 12). The Christian must learn to view his special mission in the light of this great struggle. Then when it may seem that the work of spreading the gospel is doomed to failure and the second coming of Christ is indefinitely delayed, he will remember the great controversy and all that God has accomplished so far.

He will remember how through the ages God has worked so patiently to reveal the truth about himself—and he is still working just as patiently now to win the human race. Then discouragement over delay turns to gratitude and admiration for God's infinite grace, and the believer is now himself more willing also to wait.

Moreover, John's Book of Revelation speaks of Satan's anger with those who dare to thwart his efforts to deceive the world. As he seeks to turn men against God, he is infuriated to hear the continuing testimony of those who still choose to "obey God's commandments and are faithful to the truth revealed by Jesus" (Revelation 12:17, GNT). This should help believers understand why their efforts to teach the truth have stirred up such fierce resistance.

Then, looking into the future, Revelation 13 foretells Satan's last, supreme attempt by means of deception, miracle, and force to silence the truth and establish himself as God. So severe is the struggle that John interrupts his description to say, "This calls for endurance and faith on the part of God's people" (Revelation 13:10, GNT).

In chapter 14 the apostle goes on to describe this company

of God's people as still resisting Satan's lies right up until the end. It is particularly mentioned of them that "in their mouth no lie was found" (Revelation 14:5). Even at risk of life they refuse to join the world in turning from the God of truth to worship the one Christ had called "the father of lies" (John 8:44). Instead, they persist in "keeping God's commands and remaining loyal to Jesus" (Revelation 14:12, NEB).

As the contest moves on toward its climax, God's loyal people are not just passively waiting for their Lord's promised return. They will not allow the enemy to win the world by default! Instead, they redouble their efforts to complete their original commission to spread the truth to every corner of the earth.

Again in the symbolic language of the Book of Revelation, John writes of seeing this last great effort to spread the gospel as represented by angels bringing urgent messages from heaven. In chapter 14 he particularly mentions three.

The first of these John saw "flying high in the air, with an eternal message of Good News to announce to the peoples of the earth, to every race, tribe, language, and nation.... [The angel] said in a loud voice, 'Honor God and praise his greatness! For the time has come for him to judge mankind. Worship him who made heaven, earth, sea, and the springs of water!'" (Revelation 14:6, 7, GNT).

"A second angel followed the first one, saying, 'She has fallen! Great Babylon has fallen!'" (Revelation 14:8, GNT). God's opposition has collapsed, both in corruption and in defeat!

A third angel followed the first two and in vivid language warned of the terrible consequences of believing Satan's lies and joining him in rebellion against God. Again there is a call for "endurance on the part of God's people, those who obey God's commandments and are faithful to Jesus" (Revelation 14:12, GNT).

These three messages, in the setting in which they are given, seem to sum up God's last message of invitation and warning to our world. Yet the message is not new. The Good News of the first angel is described as eternal, everlasting. It has always been the truth.

It was the truth back in eternity, even before Lucifer began to circulate his lies. It is the same truth that has held the loyalty of the majority of God's children throughout the universe. And it will remain the truth through the endless ages of eternity, the truth that is the basis for our freely given trust in God.

But what precisely is this truth, this everlasting gospel and Good News?

4   WHAT IS THE GOOD NEWS?

I t would seem most appropriate to look for an answer to this question in the Gospels of Matthew, Mark, Luke, and John. If we were able to ask one of them in person, he could well reply, "Why don't you read my book?"

No one, however, was more confident that he knew the true contents of the Good News than the apostle Paul. He made it an emphatic point to tell his readers that the gospel he was teaching was not something he had learned from Peter, James, or John—or any other of the Christian leaders. "The gospel I preach is not of human origin," he affirmed. "I did not receive it from any man, nor did anyone teach it to me. It was Jesus Christ himself who revealed it to me" (Galatians 1:11, 12, GNT).

On one occasion, when his version of the gospel was being seriously challenged, Paul was moved to make this extraordinary claim:

"If anyone, if we ourselves or an angel from heaven, should preach a gospel at variance with the gospel we preached to you, he shall be held outcast. I now repeat what I have said before; if anyone preaches a gospel at variance with the gospel which you received, let him be outcast!" (Galatians 1:8, 9, NEB).

If the apostle's language should seem too strong, the New English Bible translation of the Greek *anathema esto* ("let him be outcast!") is mild compared with the Phillips ("may he be... a damned soul!") or the Good News Translation ("may he be condemned to hell!") or The Living Bible ("let God's curse fall upon him") or the King James Version ("let him be accursed").

To say the least, Paul was profoundly convinced of the rightness of his version of the Good News and of the dire consequences of perverting the truth and turning to a different gospel. In his letter to the Romans he describes some of these disastrous consequences in considerable detail (see Romans 1:18–32).

Paul was stunned to observe the willingness of so many early Christians, recently set free by the Good News from the meaningless requirements of false religion, to return to the indignity and fear of their former bondage.

"I am astonished," he wrote to the Galatians, "to find you turning so quickly away... and following a different gospel. Not that it is in fact another gospel; only there are persons who unsettle your minds by trying to distort the gospel of Christ" (Galatians 1:6, 7, NEB).

"O you dear idiots of Galatia,..." Paul went on, "who has been casting a spell over you?" "At one time when you had no knowledge of God, you were under the authority of gods who had no real existence. But now that you have come to know God,... how can you revert to the weakness and poverty of such principles and consent to be under their power all over again?

Your religion is beginning to be a matter of observing certain days and months and seasons and years. You make me wonder if all my efforts over you have been wasted!" (Galatians 3:1; 4:8–11, Phillips).

But what could be expected of new converts when some of the leading Christians in Jerusalem were themselves compromising and contradicting the gospel of Christ? (See Acts 21:18–26.) Even Peter, in spite of his broadening experience with Cornelius, had reverted to some of his former narrow views, and Paul was moved to denounce him to his face and in public (Galatians 2:11–14).

This is the Paul who taught that love is never rude and that love never insists on having its own way (1 Corinthians 13:5). This is the Paul who was so respectful of the freedom of others that he could say of certain religious practices, "Let every one be fully convinced in his own mind" and "Why do you pass judgment on your brother?" (see Romans 14:1–10).

But when it came to the Good News and to those who would suppress or pervert it, Paul spoke out with almost frightening conviction and power. He even went so far as to suggest that the legalistic agitators who were upsetting the new converts by urging such external requirements as circumcision "had better go the whole way and make eunuchs of themselves!" (Galatians 5:12, NEB).

What is this Good News about which Paul felt so sure and which through the centuries has provoked such opposition and been so misunderstood? And what did Paul consider so serious a contradiction and perversion of the Good News that he could be moved to express himself so strongly to the Galatian believers?

I have asked many Christians to state what they understand to be the essence of the Good News. The varied replies have included much of the content of the Christian faith, from grace and the Atonement to the Second Coming and eternal life.

But one reply that I believe comes especially close to the heart of the matter is this: The Good News is that God is not the kind of person Satan has made him out to be.

That the Good News should be related to the issues in the great controversy between Christ and Satan is perhaps suggested by Paul's bold assertion that if even an angel from heaven dared to teach a different gospel, he should be held outcast. At first this seems incredibly presumptuous and dogmatic. But was it not an angel who began the circulation of misinformation about God and who still masquerades "as an angel of light" (2 Corinthians 11:14) as he seeks to deceive men into rejecting the Good News?

Since the great controversy began, it has been Satan's studied purpose to persuade angels and men that God is not worthy of their faith and love. He has pictured the Creator as a harsh, demanding tyrant who lays arbitrary requirements upon his people just to show his authority and test their willingness to obey. From Genesis to Revelation the Bible tells of Satan's unceasing efforts to pervert the truth and blacken the character of God.

But if God were as Satan has pictured him, how easily he could have blotted out his rebellious creatures and started over again! If all God wanted was unthinking obedience, how easily he could have manipulated the minds of men and angels and forced them to obey!

But love and trust, the qualities God desires the most, are not produced by force—not even by God himself.

That is why, instead of destroying or resorting to force, God simply took his case into court. In order to prove the rightness of his cause, to demonstrate that his way of governing the universe was the best for all concerned, God humbly submitted his own character to the investigation and judgment of his creatures.

Paul understood this when he exclaimed, "God must prove true, though every man be false; as the Scripture says, 'That you may be shown to be upright in what you say, and win your case when you go into court'" (Romans 3:4, Goodspeed).

The Good News is that God has won his case. Though all of us should let him down, God cannot lose his case. He has already won! The universe has conceded that the evidence is on his side, that the devil has lied in his charges against God.

"It is finished," Jesus cried (John 19:30). By the life that he lived and the unique and awful way he died, Jesus has demonstrated the righteousness of his Father and answered any question about God's character and government (see Romans 3:25, 26).

Paul was proud to be a bearer of this Good News, and he knew what it was all about—"in it the righteousness of God is revealed" (Romans 1:16, 17).

He confessed with shame that formerly he had seriously misrepresented God, even sharing Satan's picture of God to the extent of imprisoning and persecuting men and women in order to force them to obey (see Acts 8:3; 9:1, 2; Galatians 1:13).

But after he had accepted the Good News, Paul devoted the rest of his life to telling the truth. And who has written more eloquently about freedom, love, and grace—that faith is the only requirement for heaven, that we are not under law but under grace, and that Christ is the end of legalism as a way of being saved?

"Of course, don't misunderstand me," Paul seems to be saying in Romans. "Does faith abolish law? Perish the thought! Faith establishes law—by putting it in proper perspective" (see Romans 3:31). For, adopting Paul's understanding of faith, the man who really knows, loves, trusts, and admires God for his wise and orderly ways is most willing to listen and give heed to God's instructions on any subject.

"Let me tell you," continued Paul, "why our gracious Lord, who wants us to feel the joy and dignity of freedom, made so much use of law."

"Why then the law?" he wrote to the Galatians. "It was added because of transgressions" (Galatians 3:19). It was designed to be our guardian, our protector, to bring us back to a right relationship with God. Correctly understood, God's laws are no threat to our freedom. They were given solely for our best good; they all make good sense and deserve to be intelligently obeyed.

But as for those meaningless traditions that have nothing to do with the purposes of God, away with them! As Paul wrote to the Colossians: "Why... do you take the slightest notice of these purely human prohibitions—'Don't touch this,' 'Don't taste that,' and 'Don't handle the other'? 'This,' 'that,' and 'the other' will all pass away after use! I know that these regulations look wise with their self-inspired efforts at piety, their policy of self-humbling, and their studied neglect of the body. But in actual practice they are of no moral value, but simply pamper the flesh" (Colossians 2:20–23, Phillips).

Worse than that, taught and obeyed in the name of Christianity, they present the Christian's God as the arbitrary deity Satan has claimed him to be—and that is not good news.

What is it today that we Christians are trying to say about our God? Is it the truth? Is it really good news? Are we using the best ways of saying it? In spite of our best efforts, what are people actually hearing? Are there perhaps better ways to say it?

I believe that these are the most important questions facing us Christians today—for our own salvation and in order to fulfill our mission to the world. History warns that there is no justification for an easy confidence. There is a certain elusiveness about the Good News. It is not something that can be summarily stated and hammered home.

It was difficult even for God to explain the subtle though vital differences between the truth and Satan's charges. Even for him it was more effective to demonstrate the Good News than to explain it! This is why the Bible is so largely a history of God's handling of rebellion and his firm but gracious treatment of those who have been caught up in its destructive consequences.

It cost heaven an infinite price to bring us the Good News and confirm it with evidence that would stand for eternity. No wonder Paul was moved to speak so strongly in its defense. Just like the loyal angels, Paul was jealous for the character of God. To him it was unthinkable that some of his fellow ministers would, in effect, lend their support to Satan's charges by attributing even the slightest trace of arbitrariness to our gracious God.

It was this same perversion of the Good News that stirred Jesus most deeply. He was gentle with the worst of sinners—with Simon in his dastardly treatment of the woman who anointed Christ's feet; with the woman taken in adultery; even with his betrayer, Judas. But when some of the religious leaders, respected teachers of the people, denied the Good News and echoed Satan's lies about God, Christ uttered those awful words, "You are of your father the devil" (John 8:44).

There was no disagreement between Jesus and those teachers as to the existence of God, or the story of Creation, or the authority of the Ten Commandments, or which day was the Sabbath. Their disagreement was about the character of God. Jesus came to bring them the Good News, a picture of God that would enable them to go on doing many of the same things but for a different reason—a reason that would make it possible for them to be obedient and free at the same time. But they killed him rather than change their view of God—then hastened home to keep another Sabbath.

There is nothing more diabolic than to suppress and pervert the Good News about God. And this can be done even while apparently presenting Christian doctrine. As God is represented in some pulpits, the doctrine of the Second Coming is certainly not good news. The prospect of spending eternity with such a deity would be forbidding.

There are explanations of the death of Christ and of his intercession in our behalf that put God in a most unfavorable light, less gracious and understanding than his Son. Such subjects as sin, the law, the destruction of the wicked, the requirements for salvation, are sometimes presented in such a way—including the voice and manner of the preacher—as to leave the people with precisely the picture of God that Satan has been urging.

As followers of Christ, it is our desire to be counted among

God's loyal people, described in Revelation as obedient to his commandments and faithful to the truth revealed by Jesus.

But if in our eagerness to obey we may have left the impression that we worship a legalistic and arbitrary God, then we have not witnessed well to the Good News. And if by our teaching or our way of life we may have led some to think of God as the kind of person Satan has made him out to be, we have not shown ourselves to be trustworthy friends, either of them or of God.

There could be no greater privilege and honor than to be entrusted with the Good News about God. Surely the time has come that God's friends everywhere who share something of Paul's jealousy for God's reputation should speak up with more of Paul's pride and conviction as to what we believe the Good News really is.

5   FAITH IN GOD
IS NO LEAP IN THE DARK

In one of the saddest chapters in the history of the United States, the president was publicly accused by some of his closest associates of willful dishonesty and deceit.

What a spectacle for the onlooking world to see! The highest officer of one of the greatest nations on the earth charged with selfish abuse of presidential power and violation of the trust placed in him by the people he had been elected to represent.

The charges were categorically denied. In dramatic appeals to the loyalty of the people, the accusations were dismissed as the fabrication of disgruntled enemies. And out of affection for the president and respect for the high office he occupied, many of us were willing to believe his earnest claims. As citizens of the land that stamps on all its currency, "In God We Trust," we wanted so much also to honor our president as someone we could trust.

But now we know that mere denials are not enough. Though coming from the seat of highest authority and power, mere claims do not change falsehood into truth. The Creator of the universe has also been accused. By a disgruntled enemy he has been charged with selfish abuse of divine authority and willful distortion of the truth.

Mere denials are not enough to meet such accusations. Though coming from the Infinite One himself, how would we know if his claims are true? Satan has also made his claims, and with great show of authority and force.

But neither claims nor superior show of power can establish integrity or trustworthiness. Jesus warned against believing mere claims, even when apparently supported by supernatural signs. He spoke of religious leaders that would arise, making all kinds of false claims—even claiming to be Christ! And they would perform great miracles and wonders to prove the truthfulness of their claims. "But don't believe them," Jesus said (see Matthew 24:11, 23–26).

"Watch out," he warned, "and do not let anyone fool you. Many men, claiming to speak for me, will come and say, 'I am the Messiah!' and they will fool many people" (Matthew 24:5, GNT).

"My dear friends," John later advised, "do not believe all who claim to have the Spirit, but test them to find out if the spirit they have comes from God. For many false prophets have gone out everywhere" (1 John 4:1, GNT).

In his description of Satan's effort to sweep the whole world into his camp just before Christ's return, John speaks of the use of authority and force accompanied by the performance of great miracles, even making "fire come down out of heaven to earth in the sight of everyone." As a result, "all the people living on earth" are deceived "by means of the miracles"—except God's true people (see Revelation 13:8, 12–14, GNT).

Long ago Moses had warned the children of Israel not to be misled by the working of miracles. "A prophet or an interpreter of dreams may promise a miracle or a wonder, in order to lead you to worship and serve gods that you have not worshiped before. Even if what he promises comes true, do not pay any attention to him" (Deuteronomy 13:1–3, GNT).

The great controversy is not over who can perform the greatest miracles but over who is telling the truth. As the former Lucifer, Satan has seen the awesome power and majesty of God. And whenever he thinks of the One who hung the whole vast universe in space, he trembles with fear (James 2:19) and "knows that his time is short" (Revelation 12:12).

God has not been charged with lack of power but with its abuse. The controversy is over the character of God.

How can we know who is telling the truth?

When believers in Thessalonica were being misled by messages purporting to have come from Paul, the apostle warned them not to be deceived by such false claims but to "test everything; hold fast what is good" (1 Thessalonians 5:21).

When God took his case into court, he was inviting the universe to test even his claims and to believe only what proved to be true. Since the truth was on his side, he had nothing to fear from the most searching investigation. Nor was there any need for him to tamper with the evidence or to intimidate his inquirers.

All that was needed for God to win his case was the clearest possible exposure and demonstration of the truth. The more openness and light the better! Only cheats and liars are afraid of being questioned.

"Here lies the test," Jesus explained to Nicodemus. "Bad men all hate the light and avoid it, for fear their practices should be shown up. The honest man comes to the light so that it may be clearly seen that God is in all he does" (John 3:18–21, NEB).

God himself has come to the light. And the universe has clearly seen that the truth is with him. No lie has been found in the mouth of God. "How right and true are your ways!" all heaven agrees (Revelation 15:3, GNT: compare 16:7; 19:2). We can safely place our trust in him.

Surely such faith is no leap in the dark—unless one should believe that God has left us without light. And if God has really left us in the dark, without sufficient evidence of his trustworthiness, then Satan's charges have not been met, and trust in God would indeed be an unenlightened risk.

The first angel of Revelation 14 calls on all men everywhere to make up their minds about God. But he does not ask us to trust a God we do not know. The angel comes first with the everlasting truth, the eternal Good News. In the light of this evidence, do we find God worthy of our faith?

This is the faith of which the Bible speaks, the trust in God that makes it possible for him to save and heal. This is the faith described in Hebrews 11:1 as having "full confidence in the things we hope for, it means being certain of things we cannot see" (Phillips).

In the familiar wording of the King James Version, faith is defined as "the substance of things hoped for, the evidence of things not seen."

The Greek word translated "evidence" occurs very rarely in the New Testament. In secular usage it often means "testing," "scrutiny," "cross-examination," and the resulting "evidence," "proof," and "conviction." The verb form of this word is much more common in the Bible. It is used to describe the work of the Holy Spirit when he comes to "*convince* the world concerning sin and righteousness and judgment" (John 16:8). It occurs also in the explanation of the reluctance of a dishonest man to come to the light "lest his deeds should be *exposed*" (John 3:20). Paul uses the same word in his advice to the Ephesians to "take no part in the unfruitful works of darkness, but instead *expose* them" (Ephesians 5:11).

The Bible consistently associates faith in God with light, revelation, truth, evidence, testing, investigation.

Another term of special significance in the Hebrews definition of faith is the Greek word translated *substance* (meaning "substantial nature," "essence," "reality"), the choice of the King James committee here in chapter 11.

But a related meaning is "conviction," "confident assurance." And this was the preference of the King James committee when translating this same word in an earlier chapter of the same epistle. "For we are made partakers of Christ, if we hold the beginning of our *confidence* stedfast unto the end," (Hebrews 3:14). Twice in his second letter to the Corinthians Paul uses this same term to mean "confidence" (see 2 Corinthians 9:4, NEB; 11:17). Many scholars agree that this is the more appropriate meaning in Hebrews 11:1.

Near the end of the last century, archaeologists working in the Near East began discovering ancient papyrus documents which were records of business transactions, bills of sale, title deeds to property, guarantees. And the common term for these documents was none other than this Greek word translated "substance."

This discovery made it possible to understand Hebrews 11:1 to mean that faith is, as it were, a transaction entered into, a covenant, an agreement between the believer and his God.

God has much to offer us: forgiveness, healing, eternal life. But he never asks his intelligent creatures to believe anything for which he does not provide adequate evidence, and it is evidence that appeals to the reason. God does not expect us to have faith in a stranger. Instead, he first reveals himself. Through his Son, through the Scriptures, through the world of nature around us, in so many ways, he seeks to make himself well known.

If in the light of this revelation, this ample evidence about God, we should choose to trust him, to love him, to accept his gifts and direction, then we have entered into that transaction with God which the New Testament calls faith.

"To have faith is to be sure of the things we hope for, to be certain of the things we cannot see." This is the translation of Hebrews 11:1 in the 1976 American Bible Society's Good News Translation.

The 1970 Catholic New American Bible translates similarly: "Faith is confident assurance concerning what we hope for, and conviction about things we do not see."

Long before the King James Version, William Tyndale, who was burned at the stake for daring to produce the first printed English New Testament, had the insight to offer this translation: "Fayth is a sure confidence of thynges which are hoped for, and a certayntie of thynges which are not sene. "

None of us has ever seen God. But this does not mean we cannot know him. "The only Son, who is the same as God and is at the Father's side, he has made him known" (John 1:18, GNT).

Faith, as I understand it, is a word we use to describe a relationship with God as with a person well known. The better we know him, the better this relationship may be.

Faith implies an attitude toward God of love, trust, and deepest admiration. It means having enough confidence in him, based on the more than adequate evidence revealed, to be willing to believe whatever he says, to accept whatever he offers, and to do whatever he wishes—without reservation—for the rest of eternity.

Anyone who has such faith is perfectly safe to save. This is why faith is the only requirement for heaven.

A faith like this is far from blind. It is based soundly upon evidence. As Paul explains in Romans 10:17 (KJV), "Faith cometh by hearing, and hearing by the word of God."

The earlier manuscripts have the name "Christ" instead of "God." Thus Goodspeed translates the same passage, "Faith comes from hearing what is told, and that hearing comes through the message about Christ."

It adds meaning to this passage to read it in its larger setting in Paul's letter to the Romans:

"Scripture says, 'Everyone who has faith in him will be saved from shame'—everyone: there is no distinction between Jew and Greek, because the same Lord is Lord of all, and is rich enough for the need of all who invoke him. For everyone, as it says again—'everyone who invokes the name of the Lord will be saved.' How could they invoke one in whom they had no faith? And how could they have faith in one they had never heard of? And how hear without someone to spread the news? And how could anyone spread the news without a commission to do so? And that is what Scripture affirms: 'How welcome are the feet of the messengers of good news!'

"But not all have responded to the good news. For Isaiah says, 'Lord, who has believed our message?' We conclude that faith is awakened by the message, and the message that awakens it comes through the word of Christ" (Romans 10:11–17, NEB).

In Paul's day there was little opportunity for a man to read this message for himself. If he wished to learn the truth about God, it was necessary for him to go to the synagogue or church and listen as the rare and costly manuscripts of the Bible were read out loud for all to hear.

This is why the introduction to Revelation says of John's book, "This is his report concerning the message from God and the truth revealed by Jesus Christ. Happy is the one who reads this book, and happy are those who listen" (Revelation 1:2, 3, GNT).

In our own time, when Bibles are so readily available, Paul might have written instead, "Faith comes by studying the Word of God" or "Faith comes by reading the message about Christ."

Those of us who have learned to read the Bible as an inspired account of God's long and costly revelation of the truth find in its pages more than sufficient evidence for our faith. When God invites us to trust him, he is not asking us to take a chance, to risk a leap in the dark. Nor is he expecting us to accept mere claims or trust some inner feeling or some sign or miracle that Satan could counterfeit.

God is simply asking that we consider the evidence, so readily available, especially in his Word, and that we freely make up our minds whether or not we can regard him as worthy of our trust.

All this assumes, of course, that the Bible itself is true. How confident can we be that the books of the Old and New Testaments are telling us the truth? Is faith in the Bible a leap in the dark?

6   CAN THE BIBLE BE TRUSTED?

Sometimes this question is answered by repeating the familiar words of 2 Timothy 3:16 (KJV): "All scripture is given by inspiration of God." But why should we accept this sweeping claim?

I have friends in the Church of Jesus Christ of Latter-day Saints who use a special edition of the King James Version. On the title page it is described as an inspired revision by the prophet Joseph Smith. The preface states that the corrections, many of them clearly supporting Mormon beliefs, were made "by direct revelation from God."

With all due respect for the beliefs of my friends, how can I know if this claim is true? Some of my Mormon friends reply, "If you have faith, God will show you that our prophet writes the truth."

The Book of Mormon closes with a similar claim of divine authority: "And when ye shall receive these things, I would exhort you that ye would ask God, the eternal Father, in the name of Christ, if these things are not true; and if ye shall ask with a sincere heart, with real intent, having faith in Christ, he will manifest the truth of it unto you, by the power of the Holy Ghost. And by the power of the Holy Ghost ye may know the truth of all things.... And God shall shew unto you, that that which I have written is true" (Moroni 10:4, 5, 29).

I have friends who rejoice in their faith in Christ and who pray earnestly that the Holy Spirit will lead them into truth, yet who do not find it in their hearts to accept the claims of the Book of Mormon or the "inspired revision" of the King James Version. Are they therefore rejecting the truth?

Perhaps the most extraordinary Bible in my collection is a copy of the New Testament "As Revised and Corrected by the Spirits." Published in New York in 1861, it describes itself as a revision of the New Testament made by Jesus and some of the apostles, who returned "personally in the spirit" to make the needed corrections.

The preface explains that "many errors have found their way" into the Scriptures at the hands of "designing men." The "corrected" version of the Bible teaches that "resurrections means [sic] only the resurrections of the spirits"; that "heaven is a condition of happiness without regard to location"; that "the Holy Spirit from God is the spirit of some holy person which has once been in the flesh."

The preface concludes with this authoritative invitation: "Dear Reader, trust in God, who made all things after the counsel of his own will. The Holy Spirits feel much interest in this work, and the spirits who corrected it desire that the world will receive this correction as coming from them, directed by God himself, which is true." The author of the preface is then named—"Jesus, the Christ."

There is no hesitancy in the wording of this claim. Then should we believe it?

The hazard of hastily accepting claims is dramatically illustrated in the Sears, Roebuck catalog of 1902. The section on drugs offers quick relief for ailments that modern medicine is still struggling to remedy. All come with Sears' absolute guarantee.

There is Sure Cure for the tobacco habit, the liquor habit, the opium and morphine habit, and obesity. There is Mexican Headache Cure, "positively guaranteed" to relieve splitting headaches within fifteen minutes. There is Dr. Rose's French Arsenic Complexion Wafers, "perfectly harmless" and guaranteed to make anyone beautiful, "no matter what your disfigurements may be."

Then there is Dr. Hammond's Nerve and Brain Pills, "positively guaranteed" to cure an endless list of ills, even poor memory. "No matter what the cause may be or how severe your trouble is, Dr. Hammond's Nerve and Brain Pills will cure you." The hesitant customer is assured that all Sears' drugs have been prepared from prescriptions furnished by "the world's highest medical authorities," and he is warned to "beware of quack doctors who advertise to scare men into paying money for remedies which have no merit."

Sears, Roebuck would be the first today to urge its customers not to believe these incredible claims!

All around us, in the realm of religion, in the marketplace, on the television screen, we are constantly confronted with competing claims. Obviously, all of them cannot be true. We would do well to follow Paul's advice to "test everything; hold fast what is good." (1 Thessalonians 5:21).

The Bible is the most thoroughly tested book that has ever been written. By believers and skeptics alike it has been examined from cover to cover, every chapter, every verse, even every word. Thousands of volumes have been written about this Book.

It is an overwhelming experience to stand in the Biblical section of a great university library, the Library of Congress, the British Museum, and realize that a lifetime would not be nearly enough to read all that has been written through the centuries about every aspect of the Scriptures. Just the study of the thousands of Biblical manuscripts and other ancient sources of the text absorbs the continuous attention of generations of cooperating scholars around the world.

All this examination of the Bible has not led all inquirers to the same conclusions. But the research of even the most skeptical of critics has often only served to enlarge the accumulating store of information about the Book. And all this is available to the one who asks today, "Can the Bible be trusted?"

Consider again 2 Timothy 3:16: "All scripture is inspired by God." How much is to be included in the "all"?

When I look at the Bible in my New King James, the Good News Translation, the New International, or most other Protestant versions, I find a total of sixty-six books. But when I look in my Rheims-Douay, New American, Knox, or other Catholic versions, I find the same sixty-six plus a number of additional books commonly known as the Apocrypha.

Some of these apocryphal writings, such as the additions to Esther and Daniel, are woven in as integral parts of the sixty-six books. In versions used by Protestants or Jews, there are twelve chapters in the Book of Daniel and thirty verses in chapter 3. But in Catholic Bibles, Daniel has fourteen chapters and one hundred verses in chapter 3. When a devout Roman Catholic has just read for his morning devotions Daniel 14, he can turn in his Bible to 2 Timothy 3:16 and be assured that everything in his version of the Scriptures is inspired of God. Or is that the intention of this famous verse?

Jesus always seemed to express confidence in the Bible that he used. In his Sermon on the Mount, Jesus said, "Think not that I have come to abolish the law and the prophets; I have come not to abolish them but to fulfil them" (Matthew 5:17). After the Resurrection he reminded his disciples that "everything written about me in the law of Moses and the prophets and the psalms must be fulfilled" (Luke 24:44). In these two statements Jesus endorsed the books of the Old Testament as they were customarily arranged in those days.

Through the years, as the Old Testament writings appeared, they were gradually arranged into three groups or divisions.

The first five books of the Bible made up the division called the Law or the Law of Moses.

Joshua, Judges, Samuel, Kings, Isaiah, Jeremiah, Ezekiel, and the twelve minor prophets (Hosea to Malachi) made up the division called the Prophets. Sometimes, as in Matthew 5:17, the whole Old Testament was designated by the name of these first two divisions, the Law and the Prophets.

The remaining books of the Old Testament formed the third division, known as the Writings, the group referred to by Jesus as "the psalms," Psalms being the first book in this group.

The thirty-nine books in these three divisions made up the Old Testament canon. *Canon* means "measure" or "rule." A canonical book, therefore, is one that measures up to a certain standard.

In the early years of the Christian church, twenty-seven more documents came to be regarded as measuring up to the standard and were eventually arranged into the canon of the New Testament.

But the canonical sixty-six were not the only religious books in circulation that had an appearance of being Biblical. In fact, there were more books that were judged uncanonical than were accepted as authoritative. Many of these were written during the period between the Testaments and bore considerable resemblance to books already in the canon. They carried such titles as The Wisdom of Solomon, Ecclesiasticus, The Letter of Jeremiah, Judith, Tobit, Bel and the Dragon, Susanna, First and Second Maccabees, the Books of Adam and Eve, the Martyrdom of Isaiah, First and Second Enoch.

About a dozen of these came to be regarded by Jews living outside Palestine as of sufficient importance to merit inclusion with the other books of the Old Testament. Eventually they became an integral part of the Greek translation of the Old Testament that had been prepared during the third and second centuries before Christ for the Greek-speaking Jews in Egypt. This version of the Old Testament, called the Septuagint, became the widely used Bible of the early Christian church.

Some Catholic scholars who accept these extra books as belonging in the Old Testament like to point out that Timothy was a Greek (Acts 16:1). Naturally, then, he used the Septuagint; and the Septuagint contained the extra books. Consequently, when Paul wrote, "All scripture is inspired by God," he was including the extra Old Testament books as equally canonical!

It is significant, therefore, to notice that the Greek of 2 Timothy 3:16 may be translated, as in the New English Bible and other versions, "Every inspired Scripture has its use." This suggests, rather, that the apostle was reminding Timothy that, though there were many scriptures in circulation, only that scripture which is inspired of God is profitable.

Orthodox Jews—particularly those who were involved in the preservation of the Hebrew Old Testament—never accepted the extra books as canonical. They regarded them rather as "apocryphal," or "hidden," a disparaging term implying that they deserved to be withdrawn from circulation as spurious or heretical.

When the Catholic scholar Jerome was learning Hebrew in preparation for his revision of the Latin Bible in about A.D. 400, he came to agree with this judgment that the extra Old Testament books did not measure up. He urged that all those books not included in the Hebrew canon should be recognized as apocryphal.

Through the centuries many other Catholic theologians and church leaders have taken the same position as Jerome. Even Cardinal Cajetan, Luther's opponent at Augsburg in 1518, stated his agreement with the Hebrew canon and urged that the books recognized by Jerome as apocryphal not be relied upon for points of doctrine.

In spite of this, the Apocrypha still retains the same position in the Latin Bible that it occupied in the Greek Septuagint. This is true also of English translations of the Old Testament taken from the Latin rather than the original Hebrew and Aramaic. The 1382 Bible of Protestant John Wycliffe was one of these.

In his 1534 German Bible, Luther gathered the apocryphal books into a section between the Testaments and added this identification: "APOCRYPHA—that is, books which are not held equal to the Holy Scriptures and yet are profitable and good to read."

In reaction to Protestant criticism, the Catholic Council of Trent, on April 8, 1546, pronounced that with three exceptions the apocryphal books were to be accepted as sacred and fully canonical.

All of the Protestant English Bibles of the sixteenth century contained the Apocrypha where Luther had placed them. On my desk I keep a magnificent facsimile of the original King James Version, an exact twenty-pound replica of the 1611 first edition. There between the Testaments are the books of the Apocrypha. In fact, these disputed books were regularly included in Protestant English Bibles until an 1827 decision by the British and Foreign Bible Society that the rules of the society forbade its circulation of the uncanonical books. The American Bible Society came to the same conclusion.

How can a man decide for himself which books are worthy of his trust? What about all the other books judged uncanonical by Jews, Protestants, and Catholics alike? By what standard can a book be recognized as "measuring up"?

The history of the origin of the extra books provides some clues. The opinions of centuries of believers should not be overlooked. But in the last analysis nothing is so convincing as the actual reading of the books themselves.

The easiest decision can be made about the apocryphal writings patterned after the books of the New Testament. These include apocryphal gospels, acts, epistles, and revelations.

In the so-called Gospel of Thomas, written as early as the second century A.D., a story is told about the boy Jesus playing by the brook one Sabbath day and forming sparrows out of the moist clay. When his father objected to his doing this on the Sabbath, Jesus cried, "Go!" "And the sparrows took their flight and went away chirping."

On another occasion, according to this apocryphal book, a boy ran into Jesus and bumped him on the shoulder. Jesus cursed the boy, and he died. "The parents of the dead child came to Joseph and blamed him and said: 'Since you have such a child, you cannot dwell with us in the village; or else teach him to bless and not to curse. For he is slaying our children.'"

The Acts of Peter tells how Simon the sorcerer amazed the multitudes by flying over the city of Rome! But Peter prayed that he would fall down and break his leg in three places. And so he did!

The Acts of John recounts this extraordinary experience of John and the obedient bedbugs. The translation is taken from the 1965 edition of the New Testament Apocrypha by Edgar Hennecke, Wilhelm Schneemelcher, and R. McL. Wilson:

"And on the first day we arrived at a lonely inn; and while we were trying to find a bed for John we saw a curious thing. There was one bed there lying somewhere not made up; so we spread the cloaks which we were wearing over it, and begged him to lie down on it and take his ease, while all the rest of us slept on the floor. But when he lay down he was troubled by the bugs; and as they became more and more troublesome to him, and it was already midnight, he said to them in the hearing of us all, 'I tell you, you bugs, to behave yourselves, one and all; you must leave your home for tonight and be quiet in one place and keep your distance from the servants of God.' And while we laughed and went on talking, John went to sleep; but we talked quietly and thanks to him were not disturbed.

"Now as the day was breaking I got up first, and Verus and Andronicus with me; and we saw by the door of the room which we had taken a mass of bugs collected; and as we were astounded at the great number of them, and all the brethren had woken up because of them, John went on sleeping. And when he woke up we explained to him what we had seen. And he sat up (in) bed and looked at them and said, 'Since you have behaved yourselves and listened to my correction, go (back) to your own place.' And when he had said this and got up from the bed, the bugs came running from the door towards the bed and climbed up its legs and disappeared into the joints. Then John said again, 'This creature listened to a man's voice and kept to itself and was quiet and obedient; but we who hear the voice of God disobey his commandments and are irresponsible; how long will this go on?'"

A few early Christian groups accepted some of the apocryphal books of the New Testament as authoritative. But it has been the almost unanimous judgment of the entire Christian church that the extra New Testament books simply do not measure up to the dignity and good sense of the ones already adjudged canonical.

The apocryphal books of the Old Testament that have been rejected by Catholics, Protestants, and Jews alike have been called

Pseudepigrapha, meaning "falsely entitled." Many of them contain material that is obviously inferior and unworthy of a place among the writings of the great Hebrew prophets.

When one comes to the apocryphal books admitted to the Catholic canon, the decision requires more careful consideration. Some of the material, such as the stories of Bel and the Dragon, seem no more serious than anecdotes in the New Testament Apocrypha. But the Book of First Maccabees contains valuable history. Ecclesiasticus and The Wisdom of Solomon include many wise and pious sayings.

Luther objected to the Apocrypha on the ground that it taught ideas contrary to the books of the Hebrew canon. Among these were the doctrine of purgatory and the efficacy of prayers for the dead (2 Maccabees 12:43–45). He also noted the considerable emphasis upon the earning of merit by good works (Tobit 12:9; Ecclesiasticus 3:3; 2 Esdras 8:33; and others).

For my own satisfaction I have more than once read the entire available collection of Biblical and apocryphal documents as far as possible at one sitting. It takes only a long weekend, and it is well worth the effort. When I arrive at the last book of the New Testament Apocrypha, I still have fresh recollections of Genesis and Malachi, 1 Esdras and 2 Maccabees, the Book of Jubilees and the Story of Ahikar, Matthew and Revelation, the Gospel of the Hebrews and the Revelations of Peter and Paul.

Within that total setting, the sixty-six books of the Old and New Testament canons always assume a special place.

It is not that the books of the Apocrypha and Pseudepigrapha are without value. Even the most inferior tells us something of the beliefs and practices of that time. But among the sixty-six there is a measure of coherence and consistency that one would expect of documents purporting to tell the truth about God.

This is the ultimate standard of canonicity. And through the centuries the books that have met this requirement have been recognized as "measuring up."

As far as the New Testament is concerned, Catholics and Protestants largely agree that the canonical books are the traditional twenty-seven. As for the Old Testament, there would seem to be good reason to follow Catholic Jerome, Protestant Luther, and the interdenominational Bible societies in recognizing the thirty-nine books of the Hebrew canon as the ones most worthy of our trust.

These sixty-six books, some of them not yet written when Paul and Timothy worked together, all give evidence of belonging among those Scriptures described as "inspired by God," "teaching the truth," and leading to "faith in Christ Jesus" (2 Timothy 3:15, 16, GNT).

But there are other questions one might well raise about the trustworthiness of these ancient books.

7 THE TRUTH ABOUT GOD IN ALL SIXTY-SIX BOOKS

The Bible is a very ancient book, or rather an ancient collection of very ancient books. The most recent of them was written nearly two thousand years ago!

What assurance do we have that the books of the Bible read the same today as when they first appeared? And since these books were originally written in Hebrew, Aramaic, and Greek, how confident can we be that the hundreds of translations into English and a thousand other languages accurately represent the meaning of the original documents?

Fortunately, to answer these important questions there is a vast amount of readily available evidence. None of the original handwritten copies of the Biblical books is known to exist today. But painstaking comparison of thousands of subsequent copies, along with many other sources for the recovery of the original text, has led to agreement among many scholars that for all practical purposes we have in our possession the books of the Bible as they were first written.

F. G. Kenyon, one-time director of the British Museum and a man qualified by a lifetime of experience with Bible manuscripts to speak with authority about the preservation of the Scriptures, wrote this assurance on page 23 of his widely used book *Our Bible and the Ancient Manuscripts*:

"It cannot be too strongly asserted that in substance the text of the Bible is certain.... This can be said of no other ancient book in the world.... The Christian can take the whole Bible in his hand and say without fear or hesitation that he holds in it the true Word of God, handed down without essential loss from generation to generation throughout the centuries."

For 250 pages in his book Kenyon surveys the history of the transmission of the Biblical text, from the earliest manuscripts down to modern English versions. Referring to the most recent manuscript discoveries in his day, Kenyon concludes, "They have established, with a wealth of evidence which no other work of ancient literature can even approach, the substantial authenticity and integrity of the text of the Bible as we now possess it" (page 245).

Several decades have passed since this famous scholar published his frequently quoted convictions. Important manuscript discoveries since that time have only served to confirm his earlier conclusions.

As to the dependability of the hundreds of translations of the Bible, this is a matter that can be readily examined. All translations go back ultimately to one common source, the original Hebrew, Aramaic, and Greek. Therefore, all can be measured by essentially the same basic standard.

The story of the translation of the Bible is a long and colorful history. Excellent books are available on the subject, for the general reader or the most sophisticated student.

Suffice it to say that never has the Bible been so readily available in such accurate and readable translations as today. The Bible societies report that the Word of God has now been rendered into well over a thousand languages, covering almost the entire population of the globe.

How else could the Good News go to every nation under heaven, that all may have a chance to know the truth!

It makes for confidence in the versions to learn something about the men who prepared the translations and their reasons for undertaking such long and arduous work.

Tyndale risked and lost his life in his urgent desire to give the Bible to the people in their own language. Almost five hundred years ago he wrote that he "perceaved by experyence how that it was impossible to stablysh the laye people in any truth, excepte the scripture were playnly layde before their eyes in their mother tonge," "which thinge onlye moved me to translate the new testament."

The translators of the 1611 King James Version wrote in their no-longer-published preface that their purpose was to do that which "helpeth forward to the saving of soules. Now what can bee more availeable thereto, then to deliver Gods booke unto Gods people in a tongue which they understand?"

The committee of scholars, including Goodspeed and Moffatt, who prepared the 1952 Revised Standard Version, expressed this purpose in their preface: "The Bible is more than a historical document to be preserved. And it is more than a classic of English literature to be cherished and admired. It is a record of God's dealing with men, of God's revelation of himself and his will. It records the life and work of him in whom the Word of God became flesh and dwelt among men. The Bible carries its full message, not to those who regard it simply as a heritage of the past or praise its literary style, but to those who read it that they may discern and understand God's Word to men. That Word must not be disguised in phrases that are no longer clear, or hidden under words that have changed or lost their meaning. It must stand forth in language that is direct and plain and meaningful to people today. It is our hope and our earnest prayer that this Revised Standard Version of the Bible may be used by God to speak to men in these momentous times, and to help them to understand and believe and obey His Word."

The 1973 New International Version of the New Testament, published by the New York Bible Society International, closes its preface with these words: "We offer this version of the New Testament to him in whose name and for whose glory it has been made. We pray that it will lead many into a better understanding of the Holy Scriptures and a fuller knowledge of Jesus Christ the Incarnate Word, of whom the Scriptures so faithfully testify."

The 1976 Good News Translation concludes the preface by stating that "the Bible is not simply great literature to be admired and revered; it is Good News for all people everywhere—a message both to be understood and to be applied in daily life. It is with the prayer that the Lord of the Scriptures will be pleased to use

63

The
Truth
about
God
in
All
Sixty-six
Books

this translation for His sovereign purpose that the United Bible Societies has now published The Bible in Today's English. And to Christ be the glory forever and ever!"

The hundred-member team that produced the 2001 English Standard Version add these final words to their preface: "We know that no Bible translation is perfect or final; but we also know that God uses imperfect and inadequate things to his honor and praise. So to our triune God and to his people we offer what we have done, with our prayers that it may prove useful, with gratitude for much help given, and with ongoing wonder that our God should ever have entrusted to us so momentous a task."

One sometimes hears it suggested darkly that one reason for so many different versions of the Bible is that unprincipled scholars have desired to twist the words of Scripture to their own theological advantage. Such charges have usually been made by those who have had little or no experience in the difficult and delicate work of translation. The evidence does not support this accusation.

For my own satisfaction I have examined all the more influential versions of the English Bible, comparing them verse by verse with each other and with the original. I have looked especially for what might appear to be willful distortion of the text for doctrinal purposes. Such instances are so extremely rare as to make themselves conspicuous and readily noted by the student.

I have more than two hundred different English translations of all or part of the Bible in my modest collection. Among these, only a handful fail to qualify as straightforward translations of the original text.

There is, for example, a New Testament translated "from the metaphysical viewpoint." There are the ones already mentioned in the previous chapter as "revised by the spirits," or corrected "by direct revelation." Also, when a version seems to be the special possession of some religious group and contains unusual translations that are given special emphasis by the group, this is a warning to beware.

Truth needs no special version of the Book!

It is true that the versions vary in methods of translation, from very literal to very free. And the more idiomatic and unambiguous the translation, the more the version will reflect the translator's understanding of the meaning.

If the version describes itself as a paraphrase rather than a translation, as does the very popular The Living Bible, one would do well to heed the advice so candidly given by Dr. Taylor himself in his preface: "There are dangers in paraphrases, as well as values. For whenever the author's exact words are not translated from the original languages, there is a possibility that the translator, however honest, may be giving the English reader something that the original writer did not mean to say."

But there is paraphrase and interpretation to some extent in every translation, including the more literal King James. There is no way this can be avoided. Safety lies in using several versions, with a balance between the more literal and the more free, and comparing them with each other. The differences can be so instructive that I am glad for every version that I own.

As a freshman in college I decided to spend the rest of my life in the study and teaching of the Bible. That year I began to learn Greek, then later the other languages and tools for the detailed study of the Scriptures. After college I had the privilege of pursuing graduate studies in a university divinity school which at that time seemed to offer the most comprehensive program in the Biblical field.

65

*The
Truth
about
God
in
All
Sixty-six
Books*

Now, after sixty years of teaching Bible, it is still my most rewarding experience to join with a group in the book-by-book study of the entire Scriptures. About each of the sixty-six books we ask the same basic question, "What picture of God do you see in this book?"

No one is told what he ought to see or what he should believe. The Bible is God's gift to everyone. It belongs equally to us all. The same Spirit of truth who inspired the writers of Scripture stands ready to guide each student to see the true meaning. And as he leads the members of each group to new insights and clearer understanding, it is a great pleasure to be of assistance to each other.

So far it has been my privilege to take more than 140 such trips through the whole Bible. Each trip takes about a year; some have taken much longer. The groups have ranged in size from an intimate dozen to several hundred. For the first nineteen years of teaching, most of my students were preparing for the gospel ministry. Since then, most have been students of medicine, dentistry, and other healing professions.

Some of the most instructive trips through the sixty-six books have been with groups made up of faculty colleagues from the various schools in the university where I teach. Other groups have met in communities nearby and have included people from all walks of life and from the young to the very old.

No two trips through the Bible are ever the same. But there

are two basic questions that invariably arise. If the purpose of the Bible is to reveal the truth about God, why are there so few specific statements about him? And why do the Scriptures seem to contain so much apparently unimportant detail?

But what if the Bible should consist solely of God's claims about himself? On what basis would we believe them?

When John the Baptist was languishing in prison, he began to wonder if Jesus really was the Christ. He sent two of his disciples to Jesus with the question, "Are you the one who was to come or are we to look for somebody else?"

Did Jesus answer, "Indeed, I am the Christ. And I expect John to believe it"? Anyone could make this claim—even the devil himself. Only on the basis of evidence could John's serious question be given a satisfactory reply.

So Jesus answered John's disciples, "Go and tell John what you hear and see—that blind men are recovering their sight, cripples are walking, lepers being healed, the deaf hearing, the dead being raised to life and the good news is being given to those in need. And happy is the man who never loses faith in me" (Matthew 11:3–6, Phillips).

The Bible is a record of the things that God has said and done. But most of the Bible is made up of the historical details that describe the situations within which God so acted and so spoke. Without these details we would not be in a position to understand why God chose to speak and act in such a variety of ways. Details which would otherwise seem of little significance have their value in helping us to reconstruct the historical setting within which God was seeking to reveal himself to his people.

On each trip through the sixty-six books it soon becomes apparent that the same principle of interpretation that is applied to any ancient document must also be applied to the Sacred Scriptures. It was the context that determined the meaning of a passage when originally written. To the extent that we can recover the original context, we are able to recover the original meaning.

67

The
Truth
about
God
in
All
Sixty-six
Books

On a first reading of the Bible, there are many events and teachings that appear to put God in an unfavorable light. There is the fighting and killing in the Old Testament, the apparently cruel punishments, the representations of an angry God. They sometimes even seem to support Satan's charges that God is arbitrary, unforgiving, and severe.

In 1926 Joseph Lewis, an avowed atheist, described as "the Enemy of God" in his authorized biography, published a book entitled *The Bible Unmasked.* In this openly hostile volume Lewis has collected the most unpleasant stories of immorality and bloodshed he could find in the Old and New Testaments.

He includes the sad story of the Levite and his concubine told in Judges 19 and then asks the question, "What moral good can our children receive from the reading of this inhuman, brutal and degrading episode?… Can any element of this story inspire strength of character, or of duty to our fellow-men, or of anything that will elevate the moral life of man?" (pages 115, 116).

I mentioned this book years ago to one of the groups going through the sixty-six books. A premedical student made this thoughtful observation: If you should take a medical book designed for family use, cut out all the descriptions and pictures of disease, and publish these by themselves, the resulting volume would be useless, even repulsive, to the ordinary reader. But there is value in including these descriptions in the medical book, since they are presented in the setting of the remedy.

The same is true of the Scriptures. The Bible is very candid in its depiction of sin. Even the sins of the saints are honestly portrayed. Such candor only increases the credibility of the Biblical record. But these examples of the ugliness of sin never stand in isolation. If they did, they would be useless, and perhaps better never read. But in the sixty-six books of Scripture, sin is always presented in the setting of the remedy.

It is this setting that must never be overlooked. And it involves not only the immediate historical context of each recorded event but the far broader setting of the great controversy between good and evil—the charges of Satan, the answers of God, and the plan of salvation and healing.

Mindful of this total setting, the student learns to view the Bible as a whole and to relate all its parts to the one central theme, the revelation of the truth about God. As he reads on from book to book, there begins to appear a pattern of consistency behind all the stories. There gradually emerges a picture of an all-wise and infinitely gracious God who seems willing to go to any length to keep in touch with his people, to stoop and reach them where they are, to speak a language they can understand.

It has been my experience with each Bible study group that the further we read, the more we are moved with love and admiration for the One who would be willing to run such a risk, to pay such a price, in order to keep open the lines of communication between himself and his wayward children.

Our main concern is not with what happened to the Levite and that poor woman, or to Samson and Delilah, to David and Bathsheba, to Gideon and his fleece. The all-important question is, "What do these stories tell us about God?"

The great purpose of the Bible is to reveal the truth about our heavenly Father that we may be won back to him in love and trust. This truth, this everlasting Good News, is to be found in every one of the sixty-six books.

8   WHY DID JESUS HAVE TO DIE?

O f all the events recorded in Scripture, none speak so clearly of the truth about God as the life and the death of Jesus his Son.

It is not that the Old Testament had failed to bear eloquent and convincing witness to the truth. Some of the most persuasive examples of the infinite grace and trustworthiness of God are described in the first thirty-nine books. The answers to Satan's charges begin with the first page of the first book.

Paul spoke of the witness of the Old Testament to the righteousness of God (Romans 3:21). Jesus confirmed that the Old Testament had borne a true witness to himself (John 5:39; Luke 24:44). Hebrews 4:2 declares that the Good News was heard by God's people in the days of Moses.

When Paul needed to cite an example of great faith in God, he chose Abraham (see Romans 4), who lived as God's honored friend long before the first book of the Bible was written. Hebrews 11 lists many others in Old Testament times who, even under the most difficult circumstances, had seen the truth and learned to trust in God.

But there was need for still clearer demonstration of the truth. There was accusation in the great controversy that still had to be met. Even as Moses, Micah, and Isaiah joined with other prophets in speaking so well of God, they pointed forward to the day when God himself would give the ultimate answer to any lingering question about His own trustworthiness.

"In the past God spoke to our ancestors many times and in many ways through the prophets, but in these last days he has spoken to us through his Son. He is the one through whom God created the universe, the one whom God has chosen to possess all things at the end. He reflects the brightness of God's glory and is the exact likeness of God's own being, sustaining the universe with his powerful word" (Hebrews 1:1–3, GNT).

The first chapter of Hebrews goes on to emphasize that the One who came to reveal God was also God himself. "When he brings his first-born into this world of men, he says: Let all the angels of God worship him.... When he speaks of the Son, he says: Thy throne, O God, is for ever and ever" (Hebrews 1:6–8, Phillips).

In his letter to the church at Philippi, Paul clearly recognized that when Jesus was born among us as a human being, it was actually God who so humbled Himself: "He, who had always been God by nature, did not cling to his privileges as God's equal, but stripped himself of every advantage by consenting to be a slave by nature and being born a man" (Philippians 2:6, 7, Phillips).

To Nicodemus Jesus gave the simplest reason why he had

to come. "No one has ever gone up to heaven except the Son of Man, who came down from heaven" (John 3:13, GNT). That is, none of us has ever gone up to bring back the truth about God.

John in his Gospel offers a similar explanation: "No one has ever seen God. The only Son, who is the same as God and is at the Father's side, he has made him known" (John 1:18, GNT).

Phillips translates this same passage: "It is true that no one has ever seen God at any time. Yet the divine and only Son, who lives in the closest intimacy with the Father, has made him known." Or as the New English Bible puts it so beautifully, "God's only Son, he who is nearest to the Father's heart, he has made him known."

The most important story in all the sixty-six books is how the Son of God came to this earth, how he lived among us as the most gracious person the world has ever seen, how still in the prime of life he died a terrible death and then rose from the grave and returned to his heavenly Father.

What does this tell us about God? Why did Jesus come in human form? And why did he have to die?

Sometimes a Christian will answer these questions by repeating the best known verse in all the Bible, John 3:16: "For God so loved the world, that he gave his only begotten Son, that whosoever believeth in him should not perish, but have everlasting life" (KJV). Or perhaps he has memorized this text as translated in the New English Bible. In this version the words are in quotation marks, to indicate that they were spoken by Jesus himself. " 'God loved the world so much that he gave his only Son, that everyone who has faith in him may not die but have eternal life.' "

This famous verse, however, does not explain why Jesus had to die. It only tells us that God loved the world enough to give his Son.

The first mention of death in the Bible is in God's solemn warning in the Garden of Eden: "In the day that you eat of it you shall die" (Genesis 2:17).

Satan has denied the truthfulness of these words. "You will not die," he asserted to Adam and Eve. "It is perfectly safe—in fact, highly beneficial—to eat the fruit of this tree. You cannot depend on God always to tell you the truth. This is why it is not wise or safe to place full trust in Him" (see Genesis 3:1–6).

But Satan has not only denied the truthfulness of God's words of warning; he has also led to a perversion of their true meaning. The enemy of God and man, who would have us fear our heavenly Father as arbitrary, unforgiving, and severe, has led to the misunderstanding of this warning as a harsh demand for obedience under penalty of death.

What a baleful effect this distortion of the truth has had worldwide! How it has poisoned people's attitude toward God and their practice of religion! Obey, or face execution at the hands of an angry God. How could this satanic view have met with such wide acceptance?

For thousands of years men have offered sacrifice—sometimes even their own children—to win the favor of offended gods. Even in the Christian world some teach that had it not been for Christ's appeasement of a wrathful God, we would long ere this have been destroyed; and but for his Son's constant pleading in our behalf the Father could not find it in his heart to forgive and heal us sinners.

But need anything be done to persuade God to love his children?

Nothing is more emphatic in Scripture than that God has always loved—even his most wayward child. The consistent testimony of all sixty-six books is that our heavenly Father loves us as he loves his Son.

When God said, "In the day that you eat of it, you shall die," he was uttering no arbitrary threat. In love for his created beings, he was only warning of the consequences of sin.

Sin so changes the sinner that it actually results in death. Separated from the Source of life, he will surely die. Out of harmony with his Creator, he can no longer endure the life-giving glory of his presence.

This glory that surrounds God is often described in the Bible as having the appearance of fire. When God came down to Mount Sinai, "the appearance of the glory of the Lord was like a devouring fire on the top of the mountain in the sight of the people of Israel" (Exodus 24:17).

When Daniel recorded his vision of heaven, he described God's throne as "fiery flames, its wheels were burning fire. A stream of fire issued and came forth from before him" (Daniel 7:9, 10).

When Ezekiel described his vision of God in chapter 1, verses 4 to 28, he spoke repeatedly of the appearance of brightness and fire: "Such was the appearance of the likeness of the glory of the Lord" (verse 28). When he described the position of Lucifer before his fall, he pictured him standing in the very presence of God, in "the midst of the stones of fire" (Ezekiel 28:14, 16).

Even when so trusted a friend as Moses asked to see God in

his glory, the Lord replied, "My face you cannot see, for no mortal man may see me and live" (Exodus 33:20, NEB). Yet when Moses came down from talking with God in the mountain, his own face reflected so much of the divine glory that he had to wear a veil out of consideration for the people (see Exodus 34:29–35).

When God said that no man could see his face and live, he was not threatening that he would kill anyone he caught looking. To man, in his present sinful state, the unveiled glory of God would be a consuming fire.

How, then, could God save sinners? How could he come close enough to win them back to faith?

A distant offer of forgiveness would not restore the damage done. How could God make clear the truth about himself, that man might come to trust him once again and so be healed?

God's answer was to send his Son in human form. Though he is himself the very "radiance of the glory of God" (Hebrews 1:3, Phillips), Jesus "emptied himself,… being born in the likeness of men" (Philippians 2:7). He veiled the dazzling splendor of his divinity that men might come to know God without being consumed.

The universe was watching when God forgave Adam and Eve. Angels had heard God's warning of death. They had heard Satan's bold denial. Again the same question had been raised that started the war up in heaven. Who was right? Who was telling the truth—God or the former Light Bearer?

Had God permitted our first parents to reap the natural consequence of their rebellion and sin, the truthfulness of his warning would have been clearly seen and Satan's falsehood would have been exposed.

But "the Lord is... not willing that any should perish, but that all should come to repentance" (2 Peter 3:9, KJV). Instead of death he offered forgiveness and healing. In mercy he veiled the glory of his presence. Graciously he preserved the life of the sinner that he might have more time to consider the truth.

What a risk God ran of being misunderstood! Satan would not hesitate to take advantage of God's willingness to forgive as evidence supporting his evil charges. "I told you God has lied!" the devil could claim. "Sin does not result in death. You will not die."

Why did not God allow Satan and his followers to reap the full result of their sin? Would not their death have been the most effective way to halt the spread of rebellion and wipe out temptation and sin?

But the universe had never seen death. It was not yet apparent that death was the inevitable consequence of sin. There was danger that the universe would assume that God had executed his enemies, that onlooking beings would thus be led to obey him out of fear.

In spite of Satan's charges to the contrary, God does not desire the service of fear. It grieves him to see his children afraid. If we should be moved to keep God's commandments merely by fear of his power to destroy, our obedience would not speak well of our loving heavenly Father.

To remain free and unafraid of God, the universe must learn the truth about the results of sin. They must be helped to understand that the sinner's death is not execution at the hands of a vengeful God.

But does not the Bible make frequent mention of the awesome wrath of God? The third angel of Revelation 14 warns that in the end the wrath of God, unmixed with mercy, will be poured out on the heads of unrepentant sinners, and they will be consumed with unquenchable fire (Revelation 14:9-11).

What is this wrath of God? Is it like our human anger?

In the first chapter of Romans Paul describes how the wrath of God is poured out on those who reject and suppress the truth. Three times he explains that God gives up such people and turns them over to the results of their rebelliousness.

"For the wrath of God is revealed from heaven against all ungodliness and wickedness of men who by their wickedness suppress the truth. For what can be known about God is plain to them, because God has shown it to them. Ever since the creation of the world his invisible nature, namely, his eternal power and deity, has been clearly perceived in the things that have been made. So they are without excuse; for although they knew God they did not honor him as God or give thanks to him, but they became futile in their thinking and their senseless minds were darkened. Claiming to be wise, they became fools, and exchanged the glory of the immortal God for images resembling mortal man or birds or animals or reptiles.

"Therefore God *gave them up* in the lusts of their hearts to impurity, to the dishonoring of their bodies among themselves, because they exchanged the truth about God for a lie and worshiped and served the creature rather than the Creator....

"For this reason God *gave them up* to dishonorable passions....

"And since they did not see fit to acknowledge God, God *gave them up* to a base mind and to improper conduct" (Romans 1:18–28, emphasis supplied).

How consistent this is with what we know about God! Since faith and love cannot be forced, what else can God do but sadly give up those who reject him?

God's wrath, as Paul seems to describe it, is revealed by his turning away in loving disappointment from those who do not want him anyway, thus leaving them to the inevitable consequences of their own rebellious choice.

Surely no more awful sentence could be pronounced upon a sinner than for God to say, "Leave him alone."

Such a picture of God's wrath was not new with Paul. The Old Testament had taught it long before. In the sad but wonderful Book of Hosea the prophet depicts how God had so long and patiently sought to win back rebellious Israel. But the people mocked his love and spurned his every advance. What was there left for him to do but sadly give them up?

When Israel was young I came to love him,
And I called him out of Egypt to be my son.
But the more I called them
The further they went from me.
They made sacrifices to the Baals
And burnt incense to idols.
Yet it was I who taught Ephraim to walk,
Picking them up in my arms.
Yet they never knew that it was I who healed their bruises.
I led them with gentle encouragement,
Their harness was a harness of love.
I treated them like the man
Who eases the yoke to free the jaws—

Yes, I bent down to them and gave them food.

They must return to the land of Egypt
Or Assyria must be their king,
Because they have refused to turn to me.
The sword shall whirl around in their cities,
Break the defence of their gates,
And destroy them within their fortresses.
My people are bent on turning away from me;
The yoke is all they are fit for—
I can love them no more.

*How, oh how, can I **give you up**, Ephraim!*
*How, oh how, can I **hand you over**, Israel!*
How can I turn you into a Sodom!
How can I treat you like a Gomorrah!
My heart recoils within me,
All my compassion is kindled."

—Hosea 11:1-8, Phillips, emphasis supplied

Nineteen hundred years ago the Son of man came to this earth in human form to give us the clearest revelation of the truth about God that the universe will ever see. By the way that he lived and the way that he died he answered the questions, he met the accusations, he confirmed the truth—all with evidence that will stand for eternity.

He came to show how infinitely loving the Father is. He loved everyone, including little children. The disciples assumed that the Saviour was too busy to have time for boys and girls. But

Jesus said, "Let the children come to me, and do not hinder them" (Matthew 19:14). He came to show how infinitely patient the Father is. He treated everyone with utmost courtesy and understanding, even though he was often rebuffed and insulted in return. One day the disciples asked if Jesus wanted them to call down fire from heaven to consume the rejecters of his love. The Lord rebuked them for their heartless impatience. He had not come to destroy but to heal (see Luke 9:55; 19:10).

Jesus came to show how every detail of our lives is of concern to the Father. In all the excitement following the raising of Jairus' daughter, it was he who directed that they be sure to give her something to eat (see Luke 8:49–56).

Then at the end of his matchless life there came the supreme demonstration of what God is like. On Thursday evening Jesus was arrested. He was illegally tried. He was falsely accused. He was grossly insulted. But not once did he become angry; for God is like that!

Twice he was horribly beaten. All night long he was allowed no sleep, no food. But did he become irritated? Not for a moment; for God is like that!

Men made a game of hitting his wounded head. They jeered at his mysterious birth as illegitimate. They even spat in his face. But did his patience run out? Did he become angry with his tormentors? Never! For God is like that.

Even as he hung on the cross, enduring the pain of crucifixion and the mocking of those he came to save—even as he passed through the unspeakable agony of separation from his Father—he kept on praying, "Father, forgive them; for they know not what they do" (Luke 23:34).

This is the kind of person we know our God to be. For the Father is just as loving and forgiving as the Son. As Jesus said, "He who has seen me has seen the Father" (John 14:9).

Finally there came the moment upon which the security of the whole universe depended—the Son of God was about to die.

And as he died he did not ask, "God, why are you killing me? Why are you executing me?" He cried, "My God, my God, why have you forsaken me? Why have you given me up? Why have you let me go?" (see Matthew 27:46).

Though he had never been rebellious for a moment, Jesus was experiencing the consequence of sin. "For our sake he made him to be sin who knew no sin" (2 Corinthians 5:21). God was pouring out his wrath upon his Son. Because of our sins Jesus was "given up" and "handed over" (Romans 4:25), the same Greek word Paul used in Romans 1 to describe God's wrath.

There is no clearer picture of God than may be seen at the foot of the cross.

God had told the truth when he warned that the wages of sin is death. In his Son he was dying that death. But God was not executing his Son. He only "gave him up," as he will give up the wicked at the end. And though by rights we should have died, God did not ask us to prove the truthfulness of his word. He sacrificed himself in his Son.

What more could God do to warn us of our sin and win us back to faith? Surely he had shown himself infinitely worthy of our trust.

God's own character had been called in question before the universe. His warning that the wages of sin is death had been ridiculed in Eden. But not so anymore. Christ's death had clearly demonstrated the righteousness of God (see Romans 3:25, 26). God was shown to be right in what he had said (see Romans 3:4).

Christ died primarily to prove the righteousness of God in the great controversy.

As Paul explains, "God showed him publicly dying as a sacrifice of reconciliation to be taken advantage of through faith. This was to vindicate his own justice (for in his forbearance, God passed over men's former sins)—to vindicate his justice at the present time, and show that he is upright himself, and that he makes those who have faith in Jesus upright also" (Romans 3:25, 26, Goodspeed).

With this supreme demonstration of God's righteousness all questions about his character and government were settled throughout the universe. God had won his case. The issues in the great controversy had been clearly seen.

Only here on this planet were there any remaining doubts about God. Only here did anyone still believe that Satan might be right.

The day is coming soon when all will have made up their minds about God. Then our Lord will return "in flaming fire" (2 Thessalonians 1:7), and the glory of God will flash forth again throughout all creation. Those of us who trust in God will not be afraid to see him come. But all that is out of harmony with God will be consumed by the glory of his presence (see 2 Peter 3:7-12).

Even as the wicked die, God will not be angry with his unsavable children. As he watches them perish, we shall hear his cry, "How can I give you up! How can I let you go!"

9   GOD'S RESPECT FOR US SINNERS

What will it be like some day to stand in the presence of the Infinite One and realize he knows everything about us? Everything! Will it be comfortable to spend eternity with Someone who knows us so well? Will God haunt us with the memory of our sinful past?

For an answer we have only to watch how Jesus treated all kinds of sinners:

"Early next morning he returned to the Temple and the entire crowd came to him. So he sat down and began to teach them. But the scribes and Pharisees brought in to him a woman caught in adultery. They made her stand in front, and then said to him, 'Now, Master, this woman has been caught in adultery, in the very act. According to the Law, Moses commanded us to stone such women to death. Now, what do you say about her?'

"They said this to test him, so that they might have some good grounds for an accusation. But Jesus stooped down and began to write with his finger in the dust of the ground. But as they persisted in their questioning, he straightened himself up and said to them, 'Let the one among you who has never sinned throw the first stone at her.' Then he stooped down again and continued writing with his finger on the ground. And when they heard what he said, they were convicted by their own consciences and went out, one by one, beginning with the eldest until they were all gone.

"Jesus was left alone, with the woman still standing where they had put her. So he stood up and said to her, 'Where are they all—did no one condemn you?'

"And she said, 'No one, sir.'

" 'Neither do I condemn you,' said Jesus to her. 'Go home and do not sin again.' "

This is the way the story reads in J. B. Phillips' 1958 translation of the New Testament. In this edition, Mr. Phillips prints the story without comment in its familiar position in John 7:53 to 8:11. But in his 1972 revised edition, he adds a note at the end of the New Testament explaining that "this passage has no place in the oldest manuscripts of John, and is considered by most scholars to be an interpolation from some other source. Almost all scholars would agree that, although the story is out of place here, it is part of a genuine apostolic tradition."

If you are using the 1952 Revised Standard Version, you will have to look in the footnotes and read the story in very small print. The 1989 revision puts the story back in John 7:53 to 8:11, but in brackets. In the New English Bible of 1961, as also in the 1989 revision, the story is on a separate page at the end of the Gospel of John, with this note: "This passage . . . has no fixed place in our witnesses. Some of them do not contain it at all. Some place it after Luke 21:38, others after John 7:36, or 7:52, or 21:24." The

1976 American Bible Society Good News Translation leaves the
story in its traditional place but encloses it in brackets, with a
note explaining that "many manuscripts and early translations do
not have this passage." There are similar explanations in many
other versions.

Evidently the early Christians did not know what to do
with this remarkable story. Perhaps they were troubled by the fact
that Jesus seemed so willing to forgive this woman for so serious
an offense. Nevertheless, as Phillips has observed, many scholars
agree that the story bears the marks of genuineness and belongs in
the Bible. It is hardly the kind of story that would have been made
up in Jesus' day or been created by the typical manuscript copyist
in later years.

The distinguished Princeton scholar Bruce Metzger, in his
1964 The Text of the New Testament, page 223, agrees that "the
story… has all the earmarks of historical veracity; no ascetically
minded monk would have invented a narrative which closes with
what seems to be only a mild rebuke on Jesus' part."

Some religious leaders of Jesus' day brought this poor
woman to Christ in another attempt to trap him into contradicting
the teachings of the Old Testament. This was not the only such
attempt. Jesus' picture of God and his interpretation of the Old
Testament were so different from theirs that they even accused
him of heresy and of rejecting the authority of Old Testament
Scripture.

This is why Jesus had to say, "Think not that I have come to
abolish the law and the prophets; I have not come to abolish them
but to fulfil them" (Matthew 5:17). That is to say, "Think not that
I have come to do away with the teachings of the Old Testament.

On the contrary, I have come to complete them, to explain them, to show you what the Old Testament is all about." But eventually they killed him rather than accept his explanation.

Each attempt to entrap him Jesus met with his customary skill and grace. This time, to be sure that they could carry the crowds with them, the enemies of Christ made certain that they had the necessary evidence. In the hearing of the whole onlooking crowd they announced that "this woman was caught in the very act."

Then they posed their question: "You know the teaching of the Old Testament on this matter. You know the text about what ought to be done with a woman like this. Will you agree that she ought to be stoned?" And the public watched to see what Jesus would say.

He said nothing. He just bent down and began to write with his finger in the dust. A puff of wind, a few footsteps, and the record would be gone. Then his conscience-pricking words: "The one among you who has never sinned, let him throw the first stone."

Why didn't Jesus draw the whole crowd closer and say, "Let me tell you a few things about these accusers of this poor woman." Didn't they deserve to be exposed? What does it say about God that his Son did not publicly humiliate those self-righteous men?

This is what Christ came to reveal. This is the truth about God. He finds no pleasure in our embarrassment, in exposing our sins to others.

And when they had all gone, Jesus turned to the woman and gently said, "I don't condemn you either. Go home, and do not sin again." Graciously he sought to restore the dishonored woman's self-respect.

Simon, a wealthy man whom Jesus had cured of leprosy, invited Jesus and other friends to eat with him at his house. Three of Jesus' closest friends were also there: Lazarus and his sisters, Martha and Mary. Now Mary is described by Luke as "a woman who was living an immoral life in the town" (Luke 7:37, NEB).

While they were all reclining at the table, Mary brought a flask of very costly perfume and anointed Jesus' feet and wiped them with her hair. Simon watched with disapproval and thought to himself, " 'If this man really were a prophet, he would know who this woman is who is touching him; he would know what kind of sinful life she lives!'

"Jesus spoke up and said to him, 'Simon, I have something to tell you.'

" 'Yes, Teacher,' he said, 'tell me' " (Luke 7:39, 40, GNT).

Jesus then told a story of two debtors who both had been forgiven. And as he told it, Simon realized that Jesus had read his thoughts. He began to see himself as a worse sinner than the woman he had despised, and he wondered if Jesus might go on and expose him before his guests.

Nothing was more offensive to the Lord than selfrighteous accusation. But did he expose Simon? Did he say to the company, "Let me tell you about our host"?

Instead, the Lord as always did the gracious thing. He courteously accepted Mary's impulsive act. And with equal grace he corrected Simon without humiliating him before his friends. Simon must have been deeply touched!

When Jesus met the paralytic at the Pool of Bethesda, he did not humiliate or condemn him for having squandered his health in youthful indulgence. He simply asked him kindly, "Would you like to be well? Then pick up your mat and go home." Later Jesus met him and said, "You know what caused your trouble. Go and sin no more, lest something worse happen to you" (see John 5:1-15).

Picture Christ in the upper room the night before he was crucified. The twelve disciples were squabbling like children as to "which one of them should be thought of as the greatest" (Luke 22:24, GNT).

Did Jesus chide them for their folly or scold them for their unwillingness to wash each other's feet? Instead, he quietly arose, took a towel and a basin of water, and the universe watched as the Great Creator knelt down and washed a dozen pairs of dirty feet. He even washed the feet of his betrayer, Judas.

What fools the disciples were that night to miss a last chance to ask Jesus why he looked so troubled and what he meant when he said, "I will never again drink this wine until the day I drink the new wine with you in my Father's Kingdom" (Matthew 26:29, GNT)!

What a chance the disciples missed to wash the feet of the Son of God the night before he died! If only one of them had volunteered, what a memory he would have cherished for the rest of eternity!

Imagine the effect on the disciples as each in turn looked down on the head of Jesus bent over the basin and felt those strong carpenter's hands washing his feet.

Jesus could have looked up at them and said, "You don't believe my Father would be willing to do this, do you? But if you have seen me, you have seen the Father. The Father loves you just as much as I do. If you are comfortable with me, you will be comfortable with him."

Later he told them that one of them would betray him. But he didn't expose him to the whole group. And when he told Judas to go and do quickly the terrible thing he had to do, the other disciples thought he had been sent out for provisions or even to perform such a noble act as to make an offering for the poor.

Why didn't Jesus expose his betrayer before the others? Surely he deserved to be exposed. Think what it says about God that Jesus did not humiliate such a traitor!

Still later that night, out in Gethsemane, Jesus took Peter, James, and John still deeper into the Garden and there began his awesome experience of separation from his Father. Three times he came over to where the disciples were dozing, hoping for some companionship and comfort in his agony.

What a chance the disciples missed to encourage the Son of God! What if the three of them had arisen and gone back with Jesus and knelt down around him as he prayed? What a memory those three men would have had! But they slept through it all. And Jesus did not reprove them. He sympathized with them for being too tired to help.

A few hours later Peter was cursing and swearing in the courtyard to prove he was not a Christian. He did not even know this Christ!

Then the cock crowed, just as Jesus had said the night

before—right after Peter's bold speech that, though others might let him down, he would give his life for the Lord.

When Peter heard that sound, he looked to see if Jesus had noticed. Though he was on trial for his life and had suffered so much already, Jesus was more concerned about his erring disciple out there in the courtyard. He turned and looked straight at Peter.

As Peter knew God up to that time, he may well have expected to see wrath and indignation in the face of Christ. He surely deserved it! But instead he saw sorrow, disappointment, and pity—the face of the one who just the night before had knelt down and washed his dirty feet.

Peter went out and wept bitterly, so ashamed he was and so moved by the look he saw on Jesus' face (Luke 22:54–62).

A little later Judas came into the court, threw down the thirty pieces of silver, and confessed that he had betrayed innocent blood. Then he, too, looked at Jesus. He saw the same sorrow and pity that had touched Peter's heart—the face of the one who just the night before had knelt down and washed his dirty feet. Overcome, Judas went out and hanged himself (Matthew 27:3–5).

If only Judas had responded as Peter did to that look on Jesus' face! What a scene for all heaven to watch, if Judas had found where Peter was weeping and the two disciples had knelt down together and become new men!

Imagine how Peter felt all that Sabbath. What a fool he had made of himself the past twenty-four hours! Twice he had spoken so impetuously in the upper room. Twice he had disgraced himself in the Garden of Gethsemane. And then the cowardice and disloyalty while his Lord was being tried! Now Jesus was dead, and there was no chance for him to make things right.

No wonder he rushed to the tomb on Sunday morning when he heard the news that the grave was empty!

But it was Mary who had the privilege of seeing Christ first and carrying the good news to the other disciples. Mary, of all people! The woman who had so many problems and so many weaknesses, the one out of whom Jesus had to cast seven devils (see Luke 8:2). Yet it was Mary who was picked for this high privilege. Think what it says about God that Mary should be the one so highly honored.

When Mary recognized Jesus standing outside the tomb, she fell at his feet to worship him. And Jesus gently said, "Do not detain me now, for I have not yet ascended to my Father. But go and tell my brothers that I am going up to my Father and your Father, to my God and your God" (see John 20:17).

Listen to Jesus calling the disciples his brothers—the men who had let him down when he needed them the most!

When the angels confirmed Jesus' command to Mary to take the news to the disciples, they said, "Tell the disciples, and especially tell Peter, that Jesus has risen and will meet them in Galilee" (see Mark 16:7).

How Godlike it was of the angels to add, "and especially tell Peter"! The angels admire and worship God for the way he has treated sinners. How much they must have enjoyed adding, "Tell Peter"!

This is the kind of God with whom we may spend eternity. That is why, even though we all have sinned, we shall be comfortable in the presence of the one who knows us so well.

We have nothing to fear from the infinite memory of God. God is forgiveness personified. And he has promised not only to forgive us but to treat us as if we had never sinned. He will cast all our sins behind his back (Isaiah 38:17). He will "send them to the bottom of the sea!" (Micah 7:19; GNT).

There is no pretense or forgetfulness in this. God knows how we have lived. We know what sinners we have been. Angels have watched our every deed. But in spite of all this, our heavenly Father will treat us with dignity and respect as if we had always been his loyal children.

As God treats us, so we shall treat each other. This is why David will be comfortable there, in spite of his great sin. It is not because all memory of sin has been blotted out. This would require that every Bible be destroyed and all memory of what it contains. Gone would be all memory of the plan of salvation and God's merciful handling of the problem of sin!

The sins of David have been immortalized on the pages of Scripture. Rahab's former profession has been described there. So have the sins of Samson, Gideon, Moses, Jacob, and Abraham. Hebrews 11 indicates that they too will be in the kingdom. And they too will be comfortable there.

When Paul included a long list of sins at the end of Romans 1, he put gossiping right in the middle. No one will be admitted to heaven who cannot be entrusted with the knowledge of other people's sins and who will not wholeheartedly treat former sinners with full dignity and respect.

This is how it will be possible for David and Uriah to meet and not come to blows. Some day it may be our privilege to see those two men meet again for the first time in the hereafter. Think how David stole Uriah's wife and then arranged for the murder of the faithful soldier who had helped him become king (see 2 Samuel 11, 12; 1 Chronicles 11:10, 41)! Will the past be all forgotten?

Will Bathsheba, the mother of Solomon, David's son, have forgotten she once was Uriah's wife? Will the prophet Nathan have forgotten his moving appeal to the king? Will David have forgotten his confession in the fifty-first Psalm? Will we have forgotten David's prayer for a new heart that has helped many of us pray the same prayer?

Or will it be possible for David and Uriah to approach each other, look into each other's eyes, remember, and once more become friends? To me that would be far more wonderful!

Could we begin to treat each other this way here and now in this life? It is surely not natural to do so. It would be a great miracle of healing, like the miracle that happened to John. At first, Jesus called him Son of Thunder. But later John became "the beloved disciple" and wrote in his Gospel and Epistles so much about Christian love.

John watched the way Jesus received sinners, how he treated everyone with dignity and grace. Never had John seen such strength of character, and yet such tenderness; such fearless denunciation of sin, and yet such patience and sympathy. As he was moved to ever deeper admiration, John became more and more like the One he worshiped and admired.

It is true that on some very serious occasions Jesus had to call sin by its right name and publicly condemn it. One day some of the religious teachers, the ones so much trusted by the people, denounced Jesus' picture of his Father. They even told him he had a devil to be so describing God. Think of rejecting Jesus' picture of his own Father as false, even satanic! And those who opposed him were so pretentiously pious!

Under such extreme circumstances Jesus was moved to reply, "It is not I who has a devil. You are of your father the devil. He is a liar and the father of lies, and you prefer his lies about God to the truth" (see John 8:44, 48, 49). But even then there were tears in his voice.

Even in the final, awesome death of the wicked, God still reveals his respect for the freedom and individuality of his intelligent creatures. He has made it plain throughout Scripture that he is "not willing that any should perish" (2 Peter 3:9, KJV). "'As I live, says the Lord God, I have no pleasure in the death of the wicked, but that the wicked turn from his way and live; turn back, turn back from your evil ways; for why will you die, O house of Israel?'" (Ezekiel 33:11).

Like a physician, God stands ready to heal us; but he will not force us to be well. If we refuse his healing, God will respect our decision. If we insist on leaving, he will let us go. But the consequences will be terrible. And as we leave him for the last time, his cry over us will be the sad cry of Hosea, "How can I give you up! How can I let you go!" (see Hosea 11:8).

As a dramatic demonstration of his longing to save his people, God asked Hosea to marry a woman of dubious reputation. Later she left him and took up a life of prostitution. And God said to Hosea, "Go and look for your wife. Buy her back, and see if you can persuade her to stay with you and be your faithful wife from now on."

For many years God pleaded with his erring people to come back and be faithful once again. Patiently he kept on calling, "Come home, Israel, come home to the Lord your God! For it is your sins which have been your downfall. Take words of repentance with you as you return to the Lord; say to him, Clear us from all our evil." And God promised, "I will heal their unfaithfulness, I will love them with all my heart" (Hosea 14:1, 2, 4, Phillips).

The prodigal son did just this. He came home with words of repentance. And his father was so glad to see him that he didn't let him finish his confession. This is how our heavenly Father feels about every sinner who comes back, Jesus explained (see Luke 15:10–32).

But Israel in Hosea's day did not choose to come home. And God cried over them, "My people are bent on turning away from me…. How, oh how, can I give you up, Ephraim! How, oh how, can I hand you over, Israel!" (Hosea 11:7, 8, Phillips).

God will miss us if we're lost. He will miss us if we don't come home.

Think of the eternal void Lucifer will leave in the infinite memory of God.

But for many of us the revelation of the truth about our God, the picture of God presented throughout the whole of Scripture, leads us to repentance (Romans 2:4) and to faith (Romans 10:17). In trust and confidence we look forward to seeing God. We know that when he appears, though he comes in unveiled majesty and power, we shall not be afraid.

Sinners though we all have been, we shall be comfortable in his presence for all eternity.

10 WORSHIPING GOD WITHOUT FEAR

F ear God and give him glory, for the hour of his judgment has come; and worship him who made heaven and earth, the sea and the fountains of water."

This is the call of the first of the three angels in Revelation 14 (see verses 6-12). He is pictured as "flying in midheaven, with an eternal gospel to proclaim to those who dwell on earth, to every nation and tribe and tongue and people."

This gospel is the everlasting Good News that God is not the kind of person Satan has made him out to be—arbitrary, unforgiving, and severe. He is, instead, the loving heavenly Father Jesus came to reveal. Though awesome in his majesty and power, he is infinitely gracious toward all his people, especially his unruly children on this earth.

How could the angel bearing such good news speak also of fear and judgment? Would our loving Father call on his children to worship him with fear?

John taught that when a man comes to know and accept the truth about God, he no longer is afraid. He even anticipates the day of judgment without fear! Here are just a few sentences from John's description of what this truth and light can do to the person who chooses to believe:

"See how much the Father has loved us! His love is so great that we are called God's children—and so, in fact, we are."

"Whoever loves is a child of God and knows God. Whoever does not love does not know God, for God is love. And God showed his love for us by sending his only Son into the world, so that we might have life through him."

"God is love, and whoever lives in love lives in union with God and God lives in union with him. Love is made perfect in us in order that we may have courage on the Judgment Day; and we will have it because our life in this world is the same as Christ's. There is no fear in love; perfect love drives out all fear. So then, love has not been made perfect in anyone who is afraid, because fear has to do with punishment" (1 John 3:1; 4:7–9, 16–18, GNT).

Why, then, does the first angel call on us to fear God?

On many occasions in the Bible the word *fear* does not mean "terror," but rather "reverence" or "respect." Usually the intended meaning is indicated by the context.

In the twenty-third Psalm, David sings of his freedom from fear now that the Lord is his Shepherd. "Yea, though I walk through the valley of the shadow of death, I will fear no evil: For thou art with me" (Psalm 23:4, KJV). Here David is apparently using the word *fear* to mean "fright" or "anxiety." The Good News Translation renders this favorite verse, "Even if I go through the deepest darkness, I will not be afraid, Lord, for you are with me."

The same word translated "fear" is used in Psalm 128.

"Blessed is every one who fears the Lord, who walks in his ways! You shall eat the fruit of the labor of your hands; you shall be happy, and it shall be well with you" (verses 1, 2). Here the word clearly means "reverence," for it could hardly be said that frightened people are happy! The Good News Translation interprets the same passage: "Happy is the person who has reverence for the Lord."

It is in this same sense that Solomon taught that "the fear of the Lord is the beginning of wisdom" (Proverbs 9:10). That is to say, "To be wise you must first have reverence for the Lord" (GNT).

God has much to teach us. But unless we are willing to stand reverently and quietly in his presence, we cannot hear him speak. Every teacher knows that unless there is respect and order in the room, very little learning can take place.

Early in the Biblical record God came down on Mount Sinai to speak to his people. The whole mountain shook at the presence of the Lord. There was thunder and lightning, fire and smoke, and the sound of a very loud trumpet. And God said to Moses, "Keep the people back. If anyone even touches the mountain, he must die. Whether man or beast, he must be stoned or shot. Let a boundary be set around the mountain. If anyone breaks through, I shall consume him!" (see Exodus 19:10–25).

The people were terrified. "They trembled with fear and stood a long way off. They said to Moses, 'If you speak to us, we will listen; but we are afraid that if God speaks to us, we will die'" (Exodus 20:18, 19, GNT).

But Moses reassured the people that there was no need to be afraid. Moses knew the truth about God. Though he always approached him with deepest reverence and awe, he was not afraid. The people used to stand in their tent doors and watch Moses go in to meet God in the Tabernacle. And there the Lord would speak to Moses "face to face, as a man speaks to his friend" (Exodus 33:11).

Think how fearlessly but reverently Moses replied to God's offer to abandon Israel and make a great nation of him instead (see Numbers 14:11–19).

All the way from Egypt to Sinai the people had grumbled and complained, forgetting the miraculous deliverance at the Red Sea and God's generous provision of water and food. How could God gain the attention of such people and hold it long enough to reveal more of the truth about himself?

Should he speak softly to the people, in a "still small voice," as he would speak years later to Elijah at the mouth of the cave (1 Kings 19:12)? Should he sit and weep over Israel as he would centuries later, sitting on another mountain and crying over his people in Jerusalem? (See Luke 19:41–44; 13:34.)

Only a dramatic display of his majesty and power could command the reverence of that restless multitude in the wilderness. But what a risk God would thereby run of being misunderstood as a fearsome deity, just as Satan claimed him to be! Would this not be playing right into the hands of his enemy in the great controversy?

But it was either run this risk or lose contact with his people. And the Lord is not willing to let his people perish, uninstructed and unwarned. He is willing to run the risk of being temporarily feared, even hated, rather than lose touch with his children.

Parents and teachers should be well able to understand this

risk. Imagine yourself a grade-school teacher known for dignity and poise. In all your years of teaching you have never found it necessary to raise your voice to your young pupils. But now the principal has just urgently informed you at the door that the building is on fire and you must direct the children to leave the room as quickly as they can.

You turn and quietly announce that the building is on fire. But the room is very noisy following the excitement of recess. No one notices you standing there in front. Out of love for your roomful of children, would you be willing to shout? Still failing to gain their attention, would you care enough to climb on the desk, even throw an eraser or two? The children might finally notice this extraordinary sight—their gentle teacher apparently angry for the first time, shouting and gesturing as they have never seen her before! They would slip stunned into their seats, perhaps frightened at what they saw.

"Now, children, please don't go home and tell your parents that I was angry with you," you might say. "I was simply trying to get your attention. You see, children, the building is on fire, and I don't want any of you to be hurt. So let's line up quickly and march out through that door."

Which shows greater love? To refuse to raise one's voice lest the children be made afraid? Or to run the risk of being feared and thought undignified in order to save the children in your care?

The Bible is a record of the risks God has been willing to run of being thus misunderstood, of the lengths to which he has been willing to go to keep in touch with his people, to stoop and meet them where they are, to speak a language they can respect and understand.

He runs this same risk every time he disciplines his people. "For whom the Lord loveth he chasteneth" (Hebrews **12:6**, KJV). The translation "chasteneth" suggests only the idea of punishment. But the Greek word is not limited to this. It means to "educate," "train," "correct," "discipline," all of which may call for occasional punishment, but always for the purpose of instruction.

This explanation of the loving purpose of God's discipline Solomon included in his collection of proverbs.

> *My son, do not despise the Lord's discipline*
> > *or be weary of his reproof,*
> *for the Lord reproves him whom he loves,*
> > *as a father the son in whom he delights.*
> > > —Proverbs **3:11, 12**

Hebrews **12:5-11** cites this Old Testament proverb and then urges God's children not to overlook the encouraging meaning.

> *And have you forgotten the exhortation which addresses you as sons?—*
> *'My son, do not regard lightly the discipline of the Lord, nor lose courage when you are punished by him.*
> *For the Lord disciplines him whom he loves, and chastises every son whom he receives.'*
> > *It is for discipline that you have to endure. God is treating you as sons; for what son is there whom his father does not discipline? If you are left without discipline, in which all have participated, then you are illegitimate children and not sons. Besides this, we have had earthly fathers to discipline us and we*

respected them. Shall we not much more be subject to the Father of spirits and live? For they disciplined us for a short time at their pleasure, but he disciplines us for our good, that we may share his holiness. For the moment all discipline seems painful rather than pleasant; later it yields the peaceful fruit of righteousness to those who have been trained by it.

I realize now how much my own parents ran this risk of being misunderstood every time they meted out some much-needed discipline. The usual place for the administration of pun-ishment was in the front entrance hall of our two-story home in England. On one wall stood a tall piece of furniture with a mirror, places for hats and umbrellas, and a drawer in the middle for gloves. In the drawer were two leather straps. In imagination I can still hear the rattling of the handle on that drawer and the rustling of the straps as Mother made her selection. Then we would pro-ceed together toward the stairs.

After Mother was seated and the culprit had assumed the appropriate posture, it was her custom to discuss the nature and seriousness of the misdemeanor committed, all to the rhythmical swinging of the strap. The more serious the crime, the longer it took Mother to discuss it!

I cannot recall ever having thought while in that painful position, "How kind and loving of my mother to discipline me like this! How gracious she is to run the risk of being misunderstood or perhaps of causing me to hate her and obey her out of fear!" On the contrary, I seem to recall very different feelings at the time.

But when it was all over, we had to sit on the bottom stair and reflect on the experience for a while. And before we could run out and play again, we always had to find Mother where she was, and there would be hugging and kissing and reassurance that things would be better from now on.

Sometimes repentance was a little slow in coming. I can remember climbing to a higher stair so that I could look out through the stained-glass windows at the flowers around the lawn. But it was hard to stay angry for long or to go on feeling afraid. For Mother never seemed to lose her temper. We knew there was nothing she wouldn't do for us children and no limit to her willingness to listen to all we had to tell. She seemed so proud of our successes and so understanding when we failed.

Soon after Mother died I visited that bottom stair again for the first time in thirty-nine years. The stained-glass windows were still there, but the stair seemed a bit lower when I sat on it this time. Somehow I couldn't remember the pain and embarrassment at all. But I hope I shall never lose the meaning of those sessions with Mother at the bottom stair. She had helped us learn an essential truth about God. Not that we understood it right away. Mother was willing to wait. And if we had grown up fearing and hating her for those times of discipline and punishment, it would have broken her heart. But she cared enough about us to be willing to run that risk.

The message of Scripture is that we can trust God to care enough about his people to be willing to run this same risk. It is true that if we insist on going our own way, God will eventually let us go. But he does not give us up easily. He persuades; he warns; he disciplines. He would much rather speak to us quietly as he finally could to Elijah. But if we cannot hear the still small voice, he will speak through earthquake, wind, and fire.

Sometimes, at very critical moments, it has been necessary for God to use extreme measures to gain our attention and respect. On such occasions our reluctant reverence has been largely the result of fear. But God has thereby gained another opportunity to speak, to warn us again before we are hopelessly out of reach, to win some of us back to trust—and to find that there really is no need to be afraid.

Jesus said that he wants us all to be his friends (John 15:14, 15). Could this also be true of the Father? Does God regard us warmly, even respectfully, as if we were not only his children but his friends?

Philip asked Jesus about this one day: " 'Show us the Father, Lord, and we shall be satisfied.'

" 'Have I been such a long time with you,' returned Jesus, 'without your really knowing me, Philip?' " (John 14:8, 9, Phillips).

But the disciples were not asking about Jesus. They loved him. They welcomed his invitation to be his friends. They felt surprisingly comfortable in the presence of the One they worshiped as God's Son.

What they wanted to know was the truth about the God who had thundered on Mount Sinai, who had drowned the world in the Flood, who had destroyed Sodom and Gomorrah; the God who had consumed Nadab and Abihu and opened the earth to swallow up rebellious Korah, Dathan, and Abiram, who had ordered the stoning of Achan and had rained fire down from heaven on Mount Carmel.

"Jesus, could the Father be like you?"

And the Lord replied, "The man who has seen me has seen the Father. How can you say, 'Show us the Father'? Do you not believe that I am in the Father and the Father is in me?" (verses 9, 10, Phillips).

The Father is just as gracious and loving as the Son. He is just as understanding and willing to forgive. This is why Jesus could tell his disciples that when he returned to heaven it would not be necessary for him to beg the Father to do good things for them. "I need make no promise to plead to the Father for you, for the Father himself loves you" (John 16:26, 27, Phillips).

"And as for those distressing stories of discipline and death," Jesus might have continued, "you must not take them to mean that the Father is less merciful than I am. It was I who led Israel through the wilderness. The instructions to Moses were mine."

Paul understood this when he wrote, using the familiar Biblical symbol of the rock, "They all drank from the supernatural rock that accompanied their travels—and that rock was Christ" (1 Corinthians 10:4, NEB).

Some find it difficult to worship God as both infinite creator and gentle friend. When the fear is gone, when there is no display of majesty and power, reverence seems to fade away.

So long as Jesus miraculously fed the crowds, healed the sick, and raised the dead, the people were ready to worship him and crown him king. But when he answered his enemies with such gentleness, when he treated sinners with such patience and respect, when he explained that his kingdom would not be set up by force, when on Calvary he humbly submitted to such abuse, most of his followers either left or scoffed at his claim to be the Son of God.

Judas was one of those who mistook graciousness for weakness. When Jesus knelt to wash the disciples' feet, Judas despised
him for his humility. The god Judas could respect would never
degrade himself in such a manner.

Which inspires you to greater reverence and worship: the
terrifying manifestation of God's power on Mount Sinai or the
picture of the great Creator quietly weeping on the Mount of
Olives?

Which stirs you more: the fire on Mount Carmel or the still
small voice at the mouth of the cave?

Perhaps you still need the terrors of Sinai, the wind, the
earthquake, and the fire. If so, God may provide them for you. For
he cares enough to meet us where we are and speak in ways we can
understand.

But if we have moved on from Sinai to the Mount of Olives,
and nothing stirs us more than the beauty and quiet authority
of truth; if the story of Sinai and the story of Olivet have led
us to see God as both majestic king and gracious friend, then
we have learned how to worship God with reverence but without fear.

If we have allowed God to reveal himself through all the
various stories and teachings of Scripture, if we have learned to
view the Bible as a whole and relate all its parts to the one central
theme—the everlasting Good News about our gracious and trustworthy God—then we are ready to read some of the most fearsome
words in all the sixty-six books, the message of the third angel of
Revelation 14:

"And another angel, a third, followed them, saying with a

loud voice, 'If any one worships the beast and its image, and receives a mark on his forehead or on his hand, he also shall drink the wine of God's wrath poured unmixed into the cup of his anger, and he shall be tormented with fire and sulphur in the presence of the holy angels and in the presence of the Lamb. And the smoke of their torment goes up for ever and ever; and they have no rest, day or night, these worshipers of the beast and its image, and whoever receives the mark of its name' " (verses 9-11).

God must hate having to speak to us like this. But Jesus joins with his Father in sending us this message (see Revelation 1:1; 22:16). The One who said "Blessed are the meek" must have an urgent reason for warning us in such fearsome words.

The Bible has prepared us to understand the symbolic terms. The beast and its image have already been mentioned as representing God's enemies in the great controversy, and the mark as the badge of loyalty to Satan's side (see Revelation 13). The fire that lasts "for ever" has already been compared to the burning of a field of stubble (Malachi 4:1); it is like the "eternal fire" that totally consumed Sodom and Gomorrah many centuries ago (Jude 7). And lest the fearsomeness of the warning should lead us to doubt the gracious purposes of God, he sends the first and second angels with messages that prepare us for the third.

The first angel reminds of the everlasting truth. He calls on all men everywhere to make up their minds about God. Do we find the weight of evidence a sufficient basis for our faith? Can we trust and worship the One who created the whole vast universe?

The second angel reminds us of the falsity and deception of God's enemies. Every system based on Satan's lies is fallen in corruption and defeat.

Then the third angel warns of consequence. It is not God's will that any should perish. Nothing is plainer in all Scripture! But if we prefer Satan's lies to the truth, if we persist in rejecting God's every effort to save and heal, there is nothing else he can do but sadly give us up and hand us over to the awful consequence of our own rebellious choice. This is what it means to experience God's wrath unmixed with mercy at the end. And if we are not healed and ready to live in his presence again, the life-giving glory of him who is love will consume all that is out of harmony when he comes.

God would do anything to spare us from this final destruction. Think of what he has already done! But what can he do with those who are not moved by the persuasive appeals of the still small voice? What can he do with those who are not stirred by the messages of the prophets through the years—not even by the sad story of Hosea? How can he awaken those who are deaf even to the thunders of Sinai? How can he reach those who are not even touched by what happened on Calvary nor warned by the nature of Christ's death of how terrible is the ultimate consequence of sin?

Our heavenly Father is about to witness the loss of vast numbers of his children. For one last time he raises his voice. He—the gracious One, the One who would so much rather speak to us gently of the truth—raises his voice in one last awesome warning and appeal: "If you are bent on leaving me, I must let you go! But when I give you up, you will be destroyed!"

The devil would have us misunderstand this message as the words of an angry God, hardly one to be loved. But this terrible warning only serves to confirm the everlasting Good News. You could trust the God we worship to send these three final messages to the world. In these last days before the end he would not leave his children unenlightened and unwarned.

And behind the fearsome wording of the third angel's message stands the God of Hosea crying, "Why will you die? How can I give you up! How can I let you go!"

A God such as this we can worship without fear.

11   GOOD NEWS
ABOUT THE JUDGMENT

Just as a believer may be rejoicing in his freedom to worship God without fear, his eye may fall on this passage in the Epistle to the Hebrews: "For if we wilfully persist in sin after receiving the knowledge of the truth, no sacrifice for sins remains: only a terrifying expectation of judgement and a fierce fire which will consume God's enemies" (Hebrews 10:26, 27, NEB).

As he reflects on the forbidding import of these words, the believer may pause to remind himself of the encouragement in the Epistle of John that the man who has accepted the truth can look forward to the day of judgment unafraid (1 John 4:16–19). With this reassurance he is ready to read further in the passage from Hebrews.

"If a man disregards the Law of Moses, he is put to death without pity on the evidence of two or three witnesses. Think how much more severe a penalty that man will deserve who has trampled under foot the Son of God, profaned the blood of the covenant by which he was consecrated, and affronted God's gracious Spirit! For we know who it is that has said, 'Justice is mine; I will repay'; and again, 'The Lord will judge his people.' It is a terrible thing to fall into the hands of the living God" (Hebrews 10:28–31, NEB).

It seems apparent from these verses that the terrors of judgment are reserved for the sinner—particularly the one who chooses to persist in his sinning after knowing the truth. But we have all sinned, and we continue to come short of God's ideal (see Romans 3:23). Is there any good news about the judgment?

In the first place, it helps to look at the Biblical description of sin. The same apostle who speaks of approaching the judgment without fear defines sin as "the transgression of the law" (1 John 3:4, KJV). A more precise translation of John's Greek would be the one word *lawlessness.* As the Revised Standard Version puts it, "Every one who commits sin is guilty of lawlessness; sin is lawlessness."

Sin is not so much a failure to live up to this or that specified duty. It is rather a spirit of lawlessness, an attitude of rebelliousness, an unwillingness to listen to God or to heed his instructions.

But is it not true that in the day of judgment our behavior will be examined and will be measured by God's law? After reviewing the many wasted years of his life, Solomon came to this conclusion: "Fear God, and keep his commandments; for this is the whole duty of man. For God will bring every deed into judgment, with every secret thing, whether good or evil" (Ecclesiastes 12:13, 14).

John was shown the scene of the judgment. "Then I saw a

great white throne and him who sat upon it; from his presence earth and sky fled away, and no place was found for them. And I saw the dead, great and small, standing before the throne, and books were opened. Also another book was opened, which is the book of life. And the dead were judged by what was written in the books, by what they had done" (Revelation 20:11, 12).

Paul reminded believers that "we shall all stand before the judgment seat of God. . . . So each of us shall give account of himself to God" (Romans 14:10-12). And in the Epistle to the Hebrews we are advised not to forget that "there is nothing that can be hid from God; everything in all creation is exposed and lies open before his eyes. And it is to him that we must all give an account of ourselves" (Hebrews 4:13, GNT).

How much does God expect of us? Who will be judged safe to admit to his kingdom? James replies, "So speak and so act as those who are to be judged under the law of liberty" (James 2:12). As the Good News Translation puts it, "Speak and act as people who will be judged by the law that sets us free."

This liberating law is clearly identified in James' Epistle. "You will be doing the right thing if you obey the law of the Kingdom, which is found in the scripture, 'Love your neighbor as you love yourself.' But if you treat people according to their outward appearance, you are guilty of sin, and the Law condemns you as a lawbreaker. Whoever breaks one commandment is guilty of breaking them all. For the same one who said, 'Do not commit adultery,' also said, 'Do not commit murder.' Even if you do not commit adultery, you have become a lawbreaker if you commit murder" (verses 8–11, GNT).

This royal law of liberty is quite clearly the same law given to Israel amid the thunder and lightning of Mount Sinai. Sometimes it is suggested that the law of love is first found in the New Testament. But Moses taught the people, "You shall love the Lord your God with all your heart, and with all your soul, and with all your might," and "You shall not hate your brother in your heart,… but you shall love your neighbor as yourself" (Deuteronomy 6:5; Leviticus 19:17, 18). Moses went even further: "Do not mistreat foreigners who are living in your land. Treat them as you would a fellow Israelite, and love them as you love yourselves" (verses 33, 34, GNT).

When a lawyer asked Jesus, "Which is the great commandment in the law?" the Lord simply quoted the teachings of Moses (Matthew 22:34-40). Paul understood the Decalogue in the same way. After listing several of the Ten Commandments, he summarized by saying that "he who loves his neighbor has fulfilled the law.… Love does no wrong to a neighbor; therefore love is the fulfilling of the law" (Romans 13:8, 10).

Then, to help us understand the meaning of real love, Paul wrote 1 Corinthians 13. "Love is patient; love is kind and envies no one. Love is never boastful, nor conceited, nor rude; never selfish, not quick to take offence. Love keeps no score of wrongs; does not gloat over other men's sins, but delights in the truth. There is nothing love cannot face; there is no limit to its faith, its hope, and its endurance" (verses 4-7, NEB).

How the translators of the New Testament have searched for the best way to express the meaning of Paul's Greek words in this famous passage! Here is Phillips' version: "This love of which I speak is slow to lose patience—it looks for a way of being constructure. It is not possessive: it is neither anxious to impress nor does it cherish inflated ideas of its own importance.

117

Good
News
about
the
Judgment

"Love has good manners and does not pursue selfish advantage. It is not touchy. It does not keep account of evil or gloat over the wickedness of other people. On the contrary, it shares the joy of those who live by the truth.

"Love knows no limit to its endurance, no end to its trust, no fading of its hope; it can outlast anything. Love never fails."

Imagine living in a society where the life of every citizen can be described by the Ten Commandments and 1 Corinthians 13! No one ever kills or hates or lies or steals; no one even *wants* to hurt anyone else. All regard each other with unfeigned love, trust, and respect. There is no need for prisons, no police on every corner. Our wives and daughters can walk the streets alone at any hour. Everyone is perfectly safe and free.

This is why God's law is called the royal law of liberty. God is not asking us to do anything that is not for our best good. He values nothing higher than our freedom. Think of the price he has paid to give us back our freedom once again! But there can be no freedom without order and self-discipline, mutual love and complete trustworthiness.

Sin is rebellious rejection of God's law. Sin is hating, lying, stealing, cheating. Sin is arrogant insistence on having one's own way. Sin is stubborn unwillingness to listen to the healing words of our Creator. Sin, in its essence, is a spirit of lawlessness.

The only way God could admit rebels to his kingdom would be to turn heaven into a prison, to keep sinners in solitary confinement, lest they hurt and destroy each other. But we can trust God never to give up freedom. In his Son he gave his life to keep the universe free. He has no plans to become a prison warden. He has promised his loyal people a universe free from sin, a home of unthreatened safety and peace. We can trust him to insist forever on obedience to the royal law of liberty. This will not deprive us of our freedom. It *guarantees* our freedom for all eternity.

God can admit to his kingdom only people who can be trusted with all the privileges of freedom. This is why the plan of salvation offers more than just forgiveness. Heaven is not to be peopled with pardoned criminals but transformed saints. This is why Jesus told Nicodemus that he needed to be converted, to have such a change of heart and life that it would seem as if he had been born all over again (see John 3:1–10).

Jesus explained that this marvelous experience of healing is the work of the Holy Spirit, the Teacher of love and truth. And John describes how we may tell if the healing has begun: "No one born of God commits sin" (1 John 3:9). Or more precisely from the Greek: "No one who is born of God will continue to sin" (NIV). Phillips translates it: "The man who is really God's son does not practise sin." As John says in verse 6, "The man who lives 'in Christ' does not habitually sin" (Phillips).

Sin is lawlessness, rebelliousness. To continue in a state of habitual lawlessness means that one is still resisting the truth, still unwilling to trust and let God heal. But in the person who has been reborn, faith has taken the place of rebelliousness, there is love instead of lawlessness, there is a longing to be completely healed.

John explains further that we can "know that we have passed from death to life, because we love our brothers" (1 John 3:14, NIV). One of the first symptoms of the healing of salvation is

119

*Good
News
about
the
Judgment*

a new regard and love for our fellowmen. Without this love we have reason to question the genuineness of our conversion—in spite of our profession of faith in God. "If any one says, 'I love God,' and hates his brother, he is a liar; for he who does not love his brother whom he has seen, cannot love God whom he has not seen" (1 John 4:20).

My mother used to quote this verse when we children were all still at home. Since I was the oldest of four brothers, it seemed that she was usually directing these words at me. The logic always seemed inescapable.

This change that takes place in the believer is such a crucial turning point in his life that Jesus said it should be celebrated and confirmed by an appropriate ceremony. He instructed that his followers should be baptized. In fact, he made this part of his Great Commission to take the gospel to all the world (Matthew 28:19).

Paul offers his understanding of the meaning of this dramatic ceremony (see Romans 6:1–11). Baptism, he explained, represents the burial of old habits of sin, the end of rebellious lack of faith, the recognition that it cost the death of the Son of God to do away with sin. Then, just as Christ rose from the grave and returned to his Father, so the Christian rises from the water of baptism to a new way of life.

The first Christians symbolized this experience by being immersed beneath the water. Through the years other methods have been widely adopted as more convenient. It is significant to note this observation in the margin of the 1956 Catholic translation of the New Testament by Kleist and Lilly. The reference is to Paul's explanation of baptism in Romans 6:3: "St. Paul alludes to the manner in which Baptism was ordinarily conferred in the primitive Church, by immersion. The descent into the water is suggestive of the descent of the body into the grave, and the ascent is suggestive of a resurrection to a new life."

What about the believer who carelessly falls into sin, who in unguarded moments reveals some of the same old traits he so much deplored on the occasion of his baptism? Does this mean he has never been converted?

John answered this when he wrote to struggling beginners, "I write these things to you, my children, to help you to avoid sin. But if a man should sin, remember that our advocate before the Father is Jesus Christ and he is just, the one who made personal atonement for our sins" (1 John 2:1, 2, Phillips).

Even Moses, the one who talked to God face-to-face lost his temper in sinful pride just a few steps from the Promised Land. But Moses was no faithless rebel. He was one of the best friends God ever had on this sinful earth. How Moses repented of what he had done! Just when God wished to reveal himself to his grumbling people as the gracious provider of all their needs—in spite of all their ungrateful complaints—Moses by his anger misrepresented God as unforgiving and severe.

And God said to Moses, "Because… you were unfaithful to me in the presence of the people of Israel… [[and]] you dishonored me in the presence of the people,… you will not enter the land that I am giving the people of Israel" (Deuteronomy 32:51, 52, GNT).

God could not take lightly so hurtful a sin. Misrepresenting the truth about God is the most damaging of all sins. But how God comforted and honored his repentant friend! He took Moses into his confidence more than ever before as they talked together about future plans. The Bible says that God himself finally buried his old friend (Deuteronomy 34:6), then soon came back to take him up to heaven (Jude 9). Years later, when Jesus was here on his lonely mission, God asked Moses, his trusted friend, to come down and give encouragement to his Son! (See Matthew 17:1–8.)

121

*Good
News
about
the
Judgment*

This is the God we face in the judgment. By his side stands the One who was so gracious to Peter, Mary, and Simon, and even to Judas. John calls him our "advocate with the Father" (1 John 2:1). Paul describes him as interceding in our behalf (Romans 8:34; see also Hebrews 7:25).

But Jesus told his disciples there was no need for him to plead with the Father to be generous with his children. "I do not promise to intercede with the Father for you, for the Father loves you himself" (John 16: 26, 27, Goodspeed). Would Jesus be pleading with the Holy Spirit? Paul describes the third person of the Godhead as joining with the Father and the Son in working on our behalf: "Likewise the Spirit helps us in our weakness; for we do not know how to pray as we ought, but the Spirit himself intercedes for us with sighs too deep for words" (Romans 8:26).

The Good News is that the Father, the Son, and the Holy Spirit are all on our side in the judgment. As they are one with each other, so they are one with all loyal believers in meeting the accusations of our common enemy (see John 17:20–23).

For we have an enemy in the judgment. John calls him "the accuser of our brothers, who accuses them before our God day and night" (Revelation 12:10, NIV). Just as Satan accused God before the heavenly council, so he accuses God's people now. He accused Job before the heavenly council (Job 1:8–11) and Joshua, the high priest, in the presence of the Lord (Zechariah 3:1, 2).

Satan knows all the sins he has tempted us to commit, and

he can present these before the angels as evidence that we are not fit to be saved. If he is to be destroyed, he argues, justice demands that sinners should perish too.

Who would defend us against such charges? When Satan accused God, he was forced to lie. When he recounts our sins, he is telling the truth.

Paul answers this question in his letter to Rome: "If God is for us, who can be against us? Will not he who did not spare his own Son, but gave him up for us all, with that gift give us everything? Who can bring any accusation against those whom God has chosen? God pronounces them upright; who can condemn them? Christ Jesus who died, or rather who was raised from the dead, is at God's right hand, and actually pleads for us" (Romans 8:31–34, Goodspeed).

God pronounced Job a "perfect and upright" man, not because he had lived a sinless life, but because of his trust and faith. Satan was permitted to test Job to the limit, but Job could still cry in faith, "Though he slay me, yet will I trust in him" (Job 13:15, KJV). God had predicted in the hearing of the heavenly council that Job would never let him down, and Job honored the confidence God placed in him.

What God is looking for is faith. Were we to be judged, as Satan insists, on the record of our sinful lives, not one person on this planet could pass the test. God is not concerned, however, with our sinful past but with the kind of people we are now.

Have we been won back to trust him? Are we willing to listen and accept his forgiveness? Do we trust him enough to allow him to heal us? Have we, like David, welcomed the Holy Spirit

to create new hearts and right spirits within us? Could we be
trusted with the privileges of freedom and eternal life?

Has all rebelliousness gone, and has love taken its place? As
more light has come, do we always say yes to the truth? For we
have much yet to learn about our Infinite God. We may know as
little theology as the thief on the cross; but if we love, admire, and
trust in Christ as he did that crucifixion day, we are safe to admit
to the kingdom (see Luke 23:39–43). Like Mary, it will be our
greatest delight to sit at Jesus' feet and hear him tell us more about
the Father.

The people Christ cannot defend in the judgment are those
whose lives are still accurately described by the records of their sinful past. There has been no real change. They prefer darkness to
light, Satan's lies to the truth. They have rejected the Good News.
Their rebelliousness has not been healed.

Jesus explained to Nicodemus that there is nothing arbitrary
about the judgment. All depends upon how each person chooses
to respond to the truth. God longs to save each of his children, but
the decision to trust him is ours.

" 'God loved the world so much that he gave his only Son,
that everyone who has faith in him may not die but have eternal
life. It was not to judge the world that God sent his Son into the
world, but that through him the world might be saved.

" 'The man who puts his faith in him does not come under
judgement; but the unbeliever has already been judged in that he
has not given his allegiance to God's only Son. Here lies the test:
the light has come into the world, but men preferred darkness to
light because their deeds were evil. Bad men all hate the light and

avoid it, for fear their practices should be shown up. The honest man comes to the light so that it may be clearly seen that God is in all he does'" (John 3:16–21, NEB).

Later Jesus explained still further to his disciples that the question in the judgment is whether or not we have chosen to trust in God: "'When a man believes in me, he believes in him who sent me rather than in me; seeing me, he sees him who sent me. I have come into the world as light, so that no one who has faith in me should remain in darkness. But if anyone hears my words and pays no regard to them, I am not his judge; I have not come to judge the world, but to save the world. There is a judge for the man who rejects me and does not accept my words; the word that I spoke will be his judge on the last day'" (John 12:44–48, NEB).

When the judgment is finished, God turns sorrowfully away from those who still reject him as untrustworthy. Preferring to stay in darkness, they have lost the power of sight. More revelation, more persuasion, more discipline—nothing would be of any use. This is the meaning of that warning in Hebrews 10:26, 27: "If we purposely go on sinning after the truth has been made known to us,... all that is left is to wait in fear for the coming Judgment and the fierce fire which will destroy those who oppose God!" (GNT). Over such confirmed rebels the Father cries out as he did in the days of Hosea, "Like a stubborn heifer, Israel is stubborn.... Ephraim is joined to idols, let him alone" (Hosea 4:16, 17).

If this were an arbitrary, legalistic decision, lost sinners might hope to "make a deal" with God, to "plea bargain" with the Lord. Jesus predicted that some will arise in the resurrection of the wicked and be dismayed to find they are not among the saved.

They plead with the Savior, "Lord, Lord, open up for us. Did we not prophesy in your name and cast out demons in your name and do many mighty works in your name? Think of all the tithe we have paid, all the offerings we have given—enough to buy many tickets to the kingdom!"

125

*Good
News
about
the
Judgment*

But the Lord sadly replies, "I know what you have done. But you did it all for the wrong reason. You served me only because you feared me as arbitrary, unforgiving, and severe. Go away! I never knew you. We never were really friends" (see Matthew 7:21–23; 25:11, 12). And genuine friendship is the essential quality God desires in our relationship with him.

More than twenty-five hundred years ago the prophet Daniel was given a vision of the judgment in heaven, and he wrote out this vivid description:

> *As I looked,*
> > *thrones were placed*
> > > *and one that was ancient of days took his seat;*
> > *his raiment was white as snow,*
> > > *and the hair of his head like pure wool;*
> > *his throne was fiery flames,*
> > > *its wheels were burning fire.*
> > *A stream of fire issued*
> > > *and came forth from before him;*
> > *a thousand thousands served him,*
> > > *and ten thousand times ten thousand stood*
> > > > *before him;*
> > *the court sat in judgment,*
> > > *and the books were opened.*

I saw in the night visions,
and behold, with the clouds of heaven
there came one like a son of man,
and he came to the Ancient of Days
and was presented before him.
And to him was given dominion
and glory and kingdom,
that all peoples, nations, and languages
should serve him;
his dominion is an everlasting dominion
which shall not pass away,
and his kingdom one
that shall not be destroyed.

—Daniel 7:9, 10, 13, 14.

This awesome description would be terrifying if we did not know the Good News. Jesus is there, his human form reminding onlookers of what he has done to silence Satan's charges and win us sinners back to faith. And as we look at the Father seated there in his terrible majesty, there rings in our ears those wonderful words of our Lord: "If you have seen me, you have seen the Father. There is no need for me to plead with him for you, for the Father loves you just as I do myself."

We can trust God to be our friend in the judgment. As our Father he is jealous for our reputation. We need not fear those records of our sins. He would gladly dismiss them as irrelevant and out of date. All he asks of us is faith—that we love and trust him enough to let him forgive us, and heal us, and give us eternal life.

12   A REMINDER OF THE EVIDENCE

Right in the heart of the "royal law of liberty" is a command to remember the Sabbath. Is this perhaps one instance where God has placed an arbitrary requirement upon his people, just to show his authority and test their willingness to obey? But the whole message of Scripture is that there is no arbitrariness in God. Paul has explained that God's laws were given to help us, to protect us in our ignorance and immaturity, to lead us back to faith.

The first angel of Revelation 14 calls on us to worship God our Creator. This reminds us that the first mention of the Sabbath in the Bible is at the end of creation week.

How easily God could have created our world in a single instant of time! Instead, with the universe looking on, he chose to do it in six twenty-four-hour days. On the first day it was just "Let there be light." Then the second day, the third, the fourth, the fifth, as God in unhurried drama and majesty unfolded his plans for our earth.

By the sixth day this world was a beautiful place.

Where now were Satan's charges that God was selfish and severe? And look at the freedom he gave Adam and Eve, creating them in his own image, with individuality, power to think and to do. He created them able to love and trust—or to rebel and spit in his face!

God even gave Satan an opportunity to approach our first parents at the tree of the knowledge of good and evil. And God did not hide that tree in some dark corner of Eden. He placed it in the middle of the garden so that Adam and Eve would see it every time they came to eat at the tree of life (see Genesis 2:9; 3:2). Of course we could trust God not to allow his children to be tempted beyond their power to resist (see 1 Corinthians 10:13). So Satan's approaches were limited to the tree, and Adam and Eve were warned not to risk a confrontation with the wily foe.

Then God shared with us—as much as he could with created beings—some of his own creative power. He so designed it that when a man and a woman come together in love, they can give life to other beings—little people formed in the image of their human parents! "Have many children," the Creator said, "so that your descendants will live all over the earth and bring it under their control" (Genesis 1:28, GNT).

The universe saw that everything was very good. Love and admiration for God must have known no bounds. Where now were Satan's charges that God had no respect for freedom or that he made selfish use of his authority and power?

"On the sixth day God completed all the work he had been doing, and on the seventh day he ceased from all his work. God blessed the seventh day and made it holy, because on that day

he ceased from all the work he had set himself to do" (Genesis
2:2, 3, NEB).

So God and his universe celebrated the first seventh-day Sabbath. It was not man's seventh day. It was only his second. If the main purpose of the Sabbath is to provide a day of rest each week since our creation, we should be keeping Sabbath every Thursday! But that first Sabbath was *God's* seventh day. It was a day when the Creator called on the universe to celebrate with him the meaning of what he had done, to reflect on the truth that had been revealed and the falseness of Satan's charges.

It must have seemed to the angels that the great controversy had now been won. But Satan's most serious charge had yet to be denied. He had accused God of being a liar when the Creator had warned his creatures that death is the consequence of sin. The events of creation week had not dealt with this accusation. For thousands of years God waited to give his reply.

Then, at the most auspicious time, God sacrificed himself in his Son to prove the truthfulness of his word. "It is finished," Jesus cried. By Friday evening of crucifixion week, all questions in the great controversy had been fully answered. The most damaging of Satan's charges had been fully met.

And the next day was another Sabbath. As the Son of God lay resting in the tomb the whole onlooking universe paused to reflect on the truth that had been revealed during that last week of Jesus' life and to celebrate the costly victory that had been won on Calvary. Satan at last had been completely exposed. The trustworthiness of God had been eternally confirmed.

This is the Sabbath God told his people to remember. He knew we needed to pause each week to be reminded of the truth the Sabbath represents. The Sabbath is no mere test of our obedience. Caught up in the great controversy as we are, we need the message of the seventh day. As Jesus said to his disciples, "The Sabbath was made for the good of man" (Mark 2:27, GNT).

All through the Bible the meaning of the Sabbath is repeated and enlarged. When God gave the Ten Commandments on Mount Sinai, he presented the Sabbath as a memorial of creation week, a reminder that he is our Creator and we are his created beings.

But, as John and Paul explain, the One who created us was none other than Christ himself (see John 1:1–3; Colossians 1:16). The Sabbath reminds us every week that the One who came to save us is the One who made us in the beginning. The gentle Jesus who died on Calvary is also the supreme, all-powerful Creator of the universe. God did not send some subordinate to die for us. The Creator came himself, the One who is equal with God, for he is God. By keeping holy the Sabbath of creation week we acknowledge our faith in Jesus as not only our Saviour but also our Creator and our God.

What kind of person, then, is our God? Could he be as gracious and respectful of our freedom as is the Son? The reply comes every Sabbath: God is just like Christ, for Christ is God.

Many Christians observe the first day of the week as a memorial of Christ's resurrection. Surely it is a good thought on a Sunday morning to remember, This is the day on which Christ rose from the grave. And on Friday would it not be well to reflect, This is the day on which Christ was crucified? And on Thursday evening, This is the time when Christ met with his disciples in the upper room?

But the only weekly Sabbath of which the Bible speaks is the day set apart to remind us that the Person who lived among us as such a gentle man, the One who gave his life for us, is himself the One who made us, for he too is God.

Our salvation includes not just forgiveness but the healing of the damage sin has done. It is no less a miracle of creation to restore fallen human beings than it was to create them perfect in the beginning. No wonder David prayed as he did after his sad experience with Bathsheba, "Create in me a clean heart, O God" (Psalm 51:10).

When Moses repeated the Ten Commandments in the book of Deuteronomy, he mentioned the exodus rather than the creation as the reason for Sabbath observance: "Remember that you were slaves in Egypt and the Lord your God brought you out with a strong hand and an outstretched arm, and for that reason the Lord your God commanded you to keep the Sabbath day" (Deuteronomy 5:15, NEB).

This is no discrepancy in Scripture, nor a lapse of the great leader's memory. The purpose of the Sabbath is to remind us of the truth about God. He is not only our Creator but our Saviour and Redeemer as well. The One who created us free in the beginning is now exercising his creative power to release us from any kind of bondage and give us back our freedom once again.

Another way in which the Sabbath serves to remind us of the truth and to strengthen our faith in God is mentioned in Hebrews 4. There the Sabbath is described as a type and foretaste of the final rest and restoration to come. Just as God rested from his labors at the end of creation week, so there remains a "Sabbath-like rest" for the people of God.

When the children of Israel marched into the land of Canaan, they failed to enter God's rest because of lack of faith. They possessed the Promised Land, but they did not enjoy the Sabbath-like rest that trust in God can bring. Today, if we maintain our faith in God, we may begin to enjoy this rest even in this life. And we shall fully enter the Sabbath-like rest when we are admitted to the heavenly kingdom and Eden is restored.

These meanings of the Sabbath answer the great questions that stir the minds of thinking people, the basic questions of philosophy: Where have we come from? Why are we here? Where do we go after we die? And the overriding question, Is there a God? If so, what is he like? And what does he want of us people?

Where have we come from? The Sabbath has always reminded us that "in the beginning God created the heavens and the earth" (Genesis 1:1).

Why are we here? What is the great purpose of life? How do we attain to the greatest good in life? The Sabbath has always reminded us that the great purpose of life is our salvation, our restoration to the image of God by faith in the One who made us perfect in the beginning.

Where do we go after we die? The Sabbath points forward to the second coming of Christ, the final rest and restoration to come.

Is there a God? Do we know what he is like and what he wants of us people? The Sabbath reminds us of how God has revealed himself—in so many ways, but especially in his Son.

Since the Sabbath is so significant, it was only natural that the great adversary would seek to destroy it. Satan's purpose is to destroy faith in Christ, to undermine our confidence in him as the

Creator, and thus nullify the testimony of Jesus to the truth about his Father. But Satan could hardly hope to accomplish this as long as men continue to recognize all that is represented by the Sabbath. Therefore he lent his influence to the neglect of the Sabbath or to the distortion of its meaning.

I like the way Moffatt has interpreted Ezekiel 20:12: "I gave them my sabbath, to mark the tie between me and them, to teach them that it is I, the Eternal, who sets them apart." God's last message to the world is the restoration of this tie. It is not a message of legalism; it is not warning people that they must keep the Sabbath and the other commandments or else they will be destroyed. On the contrary, it is a message of love and faith. And God gave us the Sabbath to remind us every week of the convincing evidence that is the basis for such trust.

God has promised to restore our world, to give it back to his people again. As Jesus said in his Sermon on the Mount, "How blest are those of a gentle spirit; they shall have the earth for their possession" (Matthew 5:4, NEB). But before they can receive their inheritance, our earth must first pass through the fire described in the third angel's message. This "eternal" fire (see Jude 7) is so intense that Peter says "the elements shall melt with fervent heat, the earth also and the works that are therein shall be burned up" (2 Peter 3:10, KJV).

When the fire has completed the purification of our globe, God will re-create the world. Just as "in the beginning God created the heavens and the earth," so in the end he will create again. John said that he saw "a new heaven and a new earth; for the first heaven and the first earth had passed away" (Revelation 21:1).

In imagination I have pictured God creating our new world.

How do you think he will do it this time? Of course, just as in the beginning, he could create in an instant of time. But what if he should repeat the unhurried, majestic drama of that first creation week! The great controversy is over. No need now to answer Satan's charges. But, patient teacher that he is, might God want to answer questions anyone may have about that simple Genesis account?

Whatever way he chooses, one thing at least will be different. No need this time for God to create an Adam and Eve—just to throw open the gates of the City and welcome his children back to their Eden home (see Revelation 21, 22).

The prophet Isaiah looked forward to the day when God would create "new heavens and a new earth," and he pictures God's happy people assembling to worship their Creator "from one sabbath to another" (Isaiah 65:17; 66:23, KJV).

If on the first Sabbath in the new earth God should invite us to join with him and the onlooking universe in celebrating all that has been done, would we complain? Would we object that Sabbathkeeping is an arbitrary requirement just to show God's authority and test our willingness to obey?

Think of all there will be to remember! And for eternity the Sabbath will continue to remind us of the evidence.

13   GOD WAITS FOR US
TO TRUST HIM

Almost two thousand years have passed since God won his case on Calvary. Satan's lies and accusations have long ago been met. The freedom of the universe has been eternally secured. Why, then, does God still tolerate this one rebellious spot in his loyal universe? He longs to re-create our world and give it to his trusting saints. Why does he still wait?

Before Jesus left this earth to return to his heavenly Father, he told his disciples that he would come back soon. "How soon?" they asked. "Tell us, when will this happen? What will be the signal for your coming and the end of this world?" (Matthew 24:3, Phillips).

"Even the angels do not know the exact time," Jesus replied (see Matthew 24:36). "[But] set your troubled hearts at rest. Trust in God always; trust also in me.... I shall come again and receive you to myself, so that where I am you may be also" (John 14:1, 3, NEB).

One day as they sat together on the Mount of Olives Jesus

told his disciples of many signs by which they could tell when the end is near. He spoke of alarming disturbances on the earth and in the sky, of growing distrust between the nations, the rise of false religious leaders. He especially warned of those who would teach that his second coming was to be in secret. "Don't believe it," Jesus said; "for the Son of Man will come like the lightning which flashes across the whole sky from the east to the west." (Matthew 24:26, 27, GNT).

This is hardly the description of some invisible event. On the contrary, as John predicts, when Jesus returns, "every eye will see him" (Revelation 1:7).

Those who have learned to trust in God will be glad to see him come. As Isaiah wrote so long ago, "It will be said on that day, 'Lo, this is our God; we have waited for him, that he might save us. This is the Lord; we have waited for him; let us be glad and rejoice in his salvation'" (Isaiah 25:9).

But according to Revelation 13 most of the world will have turned against God. And when lost sinners look into the face of their spurned Redeemer—though he comes back in his human form (see Revelation 14:14)—they flee from him in terror, "calling to the mountains and rocks, 'Fall on us and hide us from the face of him who is seated on the throne, and from the wrath of the Lamb'" (Revelation 6:16).

Peter and Judas looked at that same gentle but majestic face. One was moved to repentance and the other to take his own life. Our Lord is not two-faced. The difference is in us. Those who have welcomed the Good News will be ready to see him—even in his glory—and yet not be afraid. But those who have despised

139

*God
Waits
for
Us
to
Trust
Him*

the truth will look at the One who died for them and, like Judas, be driven to suicide.

Of all the things that must happen before Jesus comes, he especially emphasized one. "This Good News about the Kingdom will be preached through all the world for a witness to all man-kind; and then the end will come" (Matthew 24:14, GNT). You can trust God to wait until everyone has had a chance to make an enlightened choice. You can trust him not to ask anyone to pass through the final time of trouble without an opportunity to prepare.

God has always waited patiently for his children to make up their minds. He waited for centuries for the people of Israel to respond to the invitations and warnings of the prophetic messen-gers. Not until they had resisted so long that they were beyond even the Creator's power to restore did God reluctantly give them up.

After the Israelites were taken off into Babylonian captivity, the writer of 2 Chronicles explained why God could no longer protect them: "The Lord, the God of their fathers, sent persistently to them by his messengers, because he had compas-sion on his people;… but they kept mocking the messengers of God, despising his words, and scoffing at his prophets, till the wrath of the Lord rose against the people, till there was no rem-edy" (36:15, 16).

Sometimes God's patience has been misunderstood to mean that one can go on sinning with impunity, for God is too patient and kind to bring discipline or to turn the sinner over to destruc-tive consequences. Paul warns of the error of such presumption:

"Are you, perhaps, misinterpreting God's generosity and patient mercy toward you as weakness on his part? Don't you realize that God's kindness is meant to lead you to repentance?" (Romans 2:4, Phillips).

In the days of the prophet Habakkuk the people were crying out in despair that God was doing nothing about their predicament. The prophet was sent to urge them not to give up their faith in God but to trust him enough to let him choose the best time for working out his plans. "It may seem slow in coming, but wait for it; it will certainly take place" (Habakkuk 2:3, GNT).

Peter warns that "in the last days there will come men who scoff at religion and live self-indulgent lives, and they will say: 'Where now is the promise of his coming? Our fathers have been laid to their rest, but still everything continues exactly as it has always been since the world began.'"

The apostle goes on to explain, "It is not that the Lord is slow in fulfilling his promise, as some suppose, but that he is very patient with you, because it is not his will for any to be lost, but for all to come to repentance. But the Day of the Lord will come: it will come, unexpected as a thief."

Then Peter refers to Paul's advice in Romans 2:4: "Bear in mind that our Lord's patience with us is our salvation, as Paul, our friend and brother, said when he wrote to you with his inspired wisdom" (2 Peter 3:3, 4, 9, 10, 15, NEB).

Sometimes God's graciousness has even been an embarrassment to some of his people! When the prophet Jonah was asked by the Lord to take a warning to the city of Nineveh, he first ran away. Later he reluctantly delivered his message: "In forty days Nineveh will be destroyed!" Then he sat down on a hillside nearby to watch the city come to its end.

141

*God
Waits
for
Us
to
Trust
Him*

But the people of Nineveh repented, and the city was not destroyed. Jonah angrily complained to God, "That's why I ran away. I knew you were too kind to go through with that prediction. You have made me look like a false prophet, and I'm so humiliated I could die" (see Jonah 3:4; 4:1–11).

God reasoned with frustrated Jonah: "Have you no pity for these people? Aren't you glad that they have chosen to repent?" But Jonah was more concerned about his prophetic reputation.

Paul was proud of the Good News about our gracious, forgiving God. Jonah was ashamed!

When Jesus returns, he will come to a generation of believers who have experienced Satan's last supreme attempt to deceive and destroy God's people. They will have accomplished what one third of the angels failed to do. They will have refused to be turned against God by Satan's lies. They will have been able to say with Paul, "If anyone—even an angel from heaven—should bring a different version of the everlasting Good News, he is wrong, and we will not believe it!" (See Galatians 1:8, 9.)

These are not babes in the truth. They are grown-up believers. They meet the Biblical description of Christian maturity: they have "their faculties trained by practice to distinguish good from evil" (see Hebrews 5:11–6:3). They have not only the teachable faith of a little child, which still needs much protection, but—like Job—they can stand alone. Though their faith is severely tested, they will never let God down.

They have welcomed the Holy Spirit, the Teacher of love

and truth. He has sealed and settled them so firmly in the truth that they cannot be moved (see John 14:16, 17, 26; 16:8; Ephesians 4:30). To be filled with the Spirit of love means to be filled with the Spirit of truth. The loving Christian is not weak; he is a person of strong conviction, and he speaks with the authority of truth.

God is waiting for such firm believers. In Revelation 7:1–3 his angels are pictured as mercifully holding back the final winds of strife until the minds of God's children have been unshakably settled into the truth.

The last book in the Bible frequently speaks of the marks of God's true people who will endure the time of trouble and welcome Jesus when he comes. Above all, they trust in God and are loyal to his Son. They have accepted the testimony Jesus bore about his Father. They believe that God is just as gracious as his Son. This everlasting gospel has won them back to faith.

Because of their trust in God, they gladly keep his commandments. That is, they love each other and they love their heavenly Father. Moved by the same Spirit who inspired the prophets, it is their greatest delight to join with every friend of God in bearing witness to Jesus (see Revelation 14:12; 12:17; 19:10; John 5:39).

It is the mission of the Christian church to help produce such people. In his letter to the believers in Ephesus, Paul explains Christ's purpose in establishing his church: "He appointed some to be apostles, others to be prophets, others to be evangelists, others to be pastors and teachers. He did this to prepare all God's people for the work of Christian service, in order to build up the body of Christ [a symbol for the Christian church]. And so we shall all come together to that oneness in our faith and in our knowledge of the Son of God; we shall become mature people, reaching to the very height of Christ's full stature. Then we shall no longer be children, carried by the waves and blown about by every shifting wind of the teaching of deceitful men, who lead others into error by the tricks they invent. Instead, by speaking the truth in a spirit of love, we must grow up in every way to Christ, who is the head" (Ephesians 4:11–15, GNT).

There is no closer unity than this oneness that is inherent in our faith. Growing up together in love and admiration for the same Christ and the same God, we are bound together by the very truth that sets us free! God's true church is made up of individuals who in the highest sense of freedom choose to band together for mutual encouragement and for greater efficiency in spreading the gospel to all the world.

God still waits for his children to grow up like this. He needs better spokesmen than Jonah proved to be. Reluctant teachers of the truth, moved only by fear or obligation, are themselves a sad denial of the content of the Good News. God waits for loyal people who are proud of the Good News, who "look eagerly for the coming of the Day of God and work to hasten it on" (2 Peter 3:12, NEB).

How much longer do you think God will have to wait? We can trust him to wait as long as there is hope for anyone. But we can also trust him not to wait forever. The One who reads our every thought will know when the gospel has gone to all the world and all final decisions are made. "So then," Jesus advised his disciples, "you also must always be ready, because the Son of Man will come at an hour when you are not expecting him" (Matthew 24:44, GNT).

Each passing year adds further evidence that God is not the kind of person Satan has made him out to be. Our heavenly Father is an infinitely powerful but equally gracious person who values nothing higher than the freedom, the dignity, and the individuality of his intelligent creatures that our love, our faith, our willingness to listen and obey, may be freely given. Obviously, what God desires the most is not produced by force. And so he waits.

If, like Paul, we are proud of the Good News, and we worship God for his infinitely wise and gracious ways, this will greatly affect the way we live, the way we treat each other, and the way we represent him. Our admiration for God will show in all we say and do. Like Abraham and Moses, who were called the friends of God, we shall be jealous for God's reputation. We shall want the world to see him as he really is. And we shall covet as the highest of all commendations the words of God about Job: "He has said of me what is right" (see Job 42:7).

The gospel does not end when Jesus returns. It is the everlasting truth. It will remain the basis of our faith for all eternity. From world to world through the whole vast universe there will never cease to echo the eternal Good News: Yes, you *can* trust God.

THE AUTHOR

Graham Maxwell is emeritus profes-sor of New Testament at Loma Linda University. He was born in England, attended college in California, and earned his Ph.D. in Biblical Studies, New Testament, from the University of Chicago Divinity School.

His dissertation dealt with the elements of interpretation that have entered into the translation of the New Testament, and especially Romans. Romans has continued to be a subject of research and writing ever since. Other publications include *I Want to Be Free, You Can Trust the Bible, Servants or Friends? Another Look at God,* and *Be Careful Who You Trust.*

For nineteen years he taught Bible and Biblical languages to college and ministerial students at Pacific Union College. In 1961 he moved to Loma Linda to serve as director of the division of religion and teach Bible to medical, dental, and other professional students.

His favorite course has been a year-long trip through the whole Bible to discover the picture of God in each of the sixty-six books. He has taught this course 140 times, not only in the classroom, but in churches and homes, to groups ranging in size from a dozen to 700.

People in 118 different countries have shared in this book by book study of the Bible with the help of tape recordings. But as one man wrote from the Falkland Islands, "I want you to know that I always read the book in the Bible before I listen to the tape.

Maxwell has watched the effect of such Bible study on over 10,000 people, "Something seems to happen," he says, "When people of all cultures discover in the Bible a consistent picture of God—an infinitely powerful but equally gracious Person, who values nothing higher than their freedom and friendship." That's what led to the writing of this book.